Kaleidoscope

4 Reading and Writing

Anita Sökmen
University of Washington

Daphne Mackey
University of Washington

HOUGHTON MIFFLIN COMPANY   Boston   New York

D0599438

Director of ESL Programs: Susan Maguire
Senior Associate Editor: Kathleen Sands Boehmer
Editorial Assistant: Kevin M. Evans
Project Editor: Gabrielle Stone
Senior Production/Design Coordinator: Carol Merrigan
Senior Manufacturing Coordinator: Marie Barnes
Marketing Manager: Patricia Fossi
Freelance Development Editor: Kathleen M. Smith

Cover Design: Ha Nguyen
Cover Image: Tony Craddock, Tony Stone Images.

www.hmco.com/college

Copyright © 1999 by Houghton Mifflin Company. All rights reserved.

No part of this work may be reproduced or transmitted in any form or
by any means, electronic or mechanical, including photocopying and
recording, or by any information storage or retrieval system without
the prior written permission of the copyright owner unless such
copying is expressly permitted by federal copyright law. With the exception of non-profit transcription in Braille, Houghton Mifflin is not
authorized to grant permission for further uses of copyrighted sections reprinted in this text without the permission of their owners.
Permission must be obtained from the individual copyright owners
as identified herein. Address requests for permission to make copies
of Houghton Mifflin material to College Permissions, Houghton Mifflin Company, 222 Berkeley Street, Boston, MA 02116-3764.

Printed in the U.S.A.

Library of Congress Catalog Card Number: 98-72230

ISBN: 0-395-85883-6

2 3 4 5 6 7 8 9–QF–02 01 00 99

To Süheyl and Joseph, and George and Caroline

Acknowledgments

We would like to thank our families for their support and understanding as we turned our focus to our computers. We are grateful for the feedback of colleagues and students at the University of Washington.

In particular we thank Cara Izumi, Elenor Holstein, Lesley Lin, Sujin Lee, Jung-Min Lee, Gap-Bae Kim, Jane Power, Mary Kay Seales, Jim Ward, and Nancy Ackles, for her knowledge of article use. We also appreciated the comments of reviewers: Victoria Badalamenti, LaGuardia Community College, NY; Brad Beachy, Butler Community College, KS; Ann Bliss, University of Colorado, CO; Jennie Britton, Valencia Community College, FL; Jan Jarrell, San Diego Community College, CA; Lois Spitzer, University of Nebraska, NE.

Thanks also to the people at Houghton Mifflin who have been so great to work with: Susan Maguire, Kathy Sands Boehmer, Kathy Smith, and Gabrielle Stone.

Contents

Unit 4 Surfing the Web   *106*

Unit 5 Cityscapes   *141*

Kaleidoscope 4 AT A GLANCE*

Unit	Reading	Preparing to Write	Writing	Targeting Language	Editing and Rewriting
1 On the Job	• context (1) • inference (1) • taking notes (2) • analyzing organization (2) • word forms (2, 3) • topic (3) • previewing (3) • skimming (3) • applying information (3) • categorizing vocabulary (3) • word roots (3) • main idea or specific details (3) • summarizing (3)	• analyzing the style and format of formal letters (2) • planning (2, 3) • survey (3)	• formal letter or personal essay (2) • survey report (3)	• collocations related to work (1) • ways to connect ideas (2)	• verb tense errors (2) • consistency in charts and lists (3)
2 The Living Language	• analyzing organization (4, 6) • word forms (4) • applying information (4) • analyzing information (5) • prediction (5) • context (4, 5, 6) • reference (5) • paraphrasing (5) • analyzing vocabulary (6) • main idea and specific detail (6) • summarizing by taking notes in a chart (6) • analyzing point of view (6)	• planning a response (5) • steps for writing a summary (6)	• formal request (5) • summary (6)	• ways to express demands (5) • collocations: verbs to report point of view (6)	• errors in article use (4) • sentence completeness (6)

*The numbers in parentheses refer to chapters.

Contents **ix**

Preface

Kaleidoscope 4: Reading and Writing provides advanced students with a variety of tasks designed to improve reading and writing skills. It is based on the premises that students

- need more than humanities-based types of writing experiences.
- need to develop a working vocabulary within a variety of topics.
- need to learn how to edit their own work.

Overview

Kaleidoscope 4 continues to develop student awareness of the fundamentals of academic, business, technical, and practical everyday writing. *Kaleidoscope 4*

- integrates reading and writing skills.
- focuses on vocabulary development, a key skill in both reading and writing.
- works on key reading skills that help students deal with authentic texts.
- recycles skills in a variety of ways.
- focuses on multigenre writing.
- includes **Preparing to Write** and **Editing and Rewriting** criteria that help less-experienced instructors feel comfortable with different types of writing assignments.
- uses task-based exercises as much as possible to keep students involved and to reduce the amount of wordiness in the text.
- allows each student to stay within his or her comfort level for sharing information and experiences.
- includes ideas for class activities.
- includes a **Reference** section with helpful information such as irregular verb forms, verbs that take gerunds or infinitives, and formats for formal business letters.

Features

With some variation, the chapters include these main elements and follow this general format:

Starting Point   Connects students to the topic of the chapter.

Reading	Includes exercises that focus on comprehension, skill-building, and vocabulary.
Targeting	Helps students work with vocabulary and key expressions related to a topic or a type of writing.
Writing	Includes **Preparing to Write** activities that help students develop ideas and write in a variety of formats. The length of compositions has been left open to fit the curricula of various programs.
Editing and Rewriting	Teaches students how to edit their own writing. Focuses on the most common mistakes in writing and suggests what students ought to look for as they check their work. The **Editing Checklist** includes questions for students to use in editing their peers' writing and their own writing.

Additional activities in *Kaleidoscope 4* include **Quickwriting** and suggestions for a **Class Activity** to round out many of the topics. Depending on whether writing and editing activities are done during class, each chapter will take from one to three hours of class time. For longer, more extensive reading assignments on the topics, teachers can supplement additional authentic materials or have students find readings on their own (from the Internet, newspaper, magazines, or library). It is also possible to recycle kinds of writing assignments in later units if more writing practice is needed. Exercises that have answers in the back of the book are identified with the (ANSWER KEY) icon.

Becoming self-editors can be an overwhelming task for ESL students. Therefore, we suggest training students to do multiple passes through their compositions, focusing on one type of error at a time. They will find more errors this way than if they try to find all types of mistakes in one pass. For this reason, editing exercises focus on one type of error at a time. As each type has been practiced in class, encourage students to build up a routine of multiple passes through their work in the editing stage. For example,

- one pass through to look for sentence completeness.
- one pass to focus on verb tenses.
- another pass to look at nouns: Do they need an article? Do they need to be plural?

As the term progresses, your feedback on writing will help students know what type of error they should pay most attention to.

Student Notebook

We suggest that students use a reading/writing notebook. Possible uses for the notebook include

- quickwriting as indicated in the text.
- journal writing if teachers find this activity beneficial.
- keeping track of outside reading with a reading "log" and brief notes about readings: new vocabulary, questions, and interesting ideas.
- reflecting on their progress as writers—what they have learned after completing their work in a topic.

Vocabulary Strategies

In order for students to learn the new vocabulary that they record in their notebooks, they need to use it. Here are some suggestions for helping students practice the vocabulary.

- Have students look in newspapers or magazines for vocabulary that they have studied in *Kaleidoscope 4*. Have them write the sentences they find and share them with the class.
- Have students find words in their notebooks from different chapters that could be used in a conversation. Have them write that conversation.
- Ask them to find five adjectives from their notebooks and, working in small groups, determine the opposites. Have them make a matching exercise to give to other groups.
- Suggest that students look through the vocabulary in their notebooks for words that are related in meaning. They can then make up related word lists with one word that doesn't fit. Then have them write sentences or paragraphs using some of the related words.
- Ask students to choose phrasal verbs (verbs with prepositions) or collocations (groups of words that go together) from the vocabulary in their notebooks. Have them write sentences with these

expressions, leaving a blank for one of the words in the expression. They can then take turns quizzing the other students on the missing words.

- Have students make flash cards by writing words and short definitions on opposite sides of index cards to practice with or use in a game.
- Create a vocabulary search game by giving students a certain amount of time to find words in their notebooks related to work, exercise, family, and other topics.
- Have students list nouns from their notebooks and use dictionaries to find the other forms in that word family. Students can teach these forms to the class.
- Ask students to find words that have the same suffix, prefix, or root. Have them compile the results in a table.
- Have students make drawings to represent words from their notebooks and ask classmates to guess the words.
- Have students work in groups to make a crossword puzzle of words from their notebooks. Then they can exchange their puzzles with classmates.
- In a game of word clues, have students choose words from their notebooks and write them on slips of paper. Working in pairs, each student chooses a word and gives clues about it to his or her partner, who tries to guess the word. After five minutes, have them change roles or switch partners.
- In group brainstorming, have students think of synonyms for words from their notebooks. They may use a dictionary. Have them make a scrambled list of the synonyms and use them for a matching quiz. Do the same for antonyms.
- Have students choose five words from their notebooks and survey native speakers for the first word that comes to mind when they hear the target word. Ask them to share the word association results with the rest of the class.

1) On the Job

When people make choices about careers, they usually think about which jobs will be in demand in the future. Although employment practices vary from country to country, people who are looking for a job usually consider a cover letter, a resume, and an interview as important parts of their job search.

Here are some of the activities you will do in this unit:

- Read about top jobs for the twenty-first century
- Read tips for finding a job
- Study vocabulary related to work
- Look at resumes and cover letters
- Read about differences in hiring and employment practices
- Write a formal cover letter or a personal essay
- Read a description of government legislation about accommodations for people with disabilities
- Write a survey report

Chapter 1

A Job for You?

When people think about careers, they usually need to balance their interests and talents with the realities of the job market. This chapter includes a chart and an article that someone thinking about a career might find helpful.

Starting Point

The Top 10

What jobs will be needed in the future? Here is a list of ten jobs that will be needed in the twenty-first century.

1. *Look at the chart of the jobs for the future. Match the job description below and on page 3 with the job. Write the letter of the job description on the chart.*

Top 10 Jobs for the Future

1. **Computer engineer**

2. **Computer systems analyst**

3. **Physical therapist**

4. **Special education teacher**

5. **Private detective and investigator**

6. **Radiologic technologist and technician**

7. **Paralegal and legal assistant**

8. **Teacher** (preschool and kindergarten)

9. **Entertainer**

10. **Secretary** (legal and medical)

Job Description

    a. Works with children with special needs
    b. Teaches 4- and 5-year-olds
    c. Acts, sings, or dances
    d. Designs computer equipment (hardware)
    e. Works with X-ray equipment used in medical diagnosis

f. Assists with legal work that doesn't require a full law degree
   g. Provides clerical office support for lawyers or doctors
   h. Sets up, maintains, and troubleshoots problems with software
   i. Works with people with physical limitations to improve their ability to get around
   j. Works for companies or private individuals to find out information about people's backgrounds

2. *Discuss these questions with a classmate.*

   a. Were you surprised by which jobs are going to be needed? What changes in technology, the workplace, or society may be related to the jobs in the list?
   b. Which jobs might pay the highest salaries? Have the highest status?
   c. Which jobs in the chart require strong communication skills? Which require strong technical skills?
   d. Would you want to have any of these jobs?

Reading

Tips Help Graduates Find Jobs

Graduates from colleges or training programs face the challenge of job hunting. These pointers can benefit graduates—or anyone who's looking for a job.

1. *Read the following article.*

Tips Help Graduates Find Jobs

1. Tell everyone you meet about your goals and what you want to do. You never can tell who they might know.

2. Don't be afraid to pick up the phone and call employers. What's the worst thing that can happen? They can say, "No." Big deal.

3. Always get a contact name. Cover letters addressed "To whom it may concern…" will probably end up in the trash.

4. There are no perfect interview answers. Employers simply want to see whether you can hold an intelligent conversation.

5. Don't worry if your grades are less than stellar. Most employers don't care if you made a C plus in history your sophomore year. They want people who are bright and willing to learn.

6. Be persistent. Don't take "No" for an answer too easily. Employers are busy and might not have focused on you.

7. You must follow up.

8. Treat secretaries and assistants with respect. They hold real power.

9. Be yourself.

10. Mass mailing 500 resumes and waiting for the phone to ring is not a job search.

11. Use the Internet. Richard Nelson Bolles includes 80 pages of career-related Web sites in his popular book, *What Color is Your Parachute?* Or you can buy *Job Hunting on the Internet* separately for $4.95.

ANSWER KEY

2. *Match the words on the left with their definition on the right. Write the number on the line. If you don't know the answer, check **the words in context** in "Tips Help Graduates Find Jobs."*

a. _____ goals		**1.**	something serious
b. _____ pick up		**2.**	continuing despite problems
c. _____ big deal		**3.**	act toward
d. _____ contact		**4.**	not let something be forgotten
e. _____ trash		**5.**	start to use
f. _____ bright		**6.**	garbage
g. _____ stellar		**7.**	to get in touch with
h. _____ persistent		**8.**	polite consideration
i. _____ focused		**9.**	objectives
j. _____ follow up		**10.**	shining like a star; fantastic
k. _____ treat		**11.**	concentrated on
l. _____ respect		**12.**	intelligent
m. _____ mass		**13.**	a large amount

ANSWER KEY

3. *Complete the sentences with words from the left-hand column in exercise 2.*

a. It's important to show _____ for someone who is older.

b. Television and radio are examples of _____ communication; they both reach lots of people.

c. I asked my friend, "What's the _____? I don't see any problem with this."

d. I just started college. I don't know what I want to major in, and I don't have any clear career _____.

e. You have to be _____ to find a good job. You can't give up.

f. I've heard that company is a great place to work because they _____ their employees so well.

4. An **inference** is something you understand from a reading, but the writer doesn't state directly. Use inference to decide which of the following job-search ideas are good ones. Put a check (✓) next to the items.

ANSWER KEY

a. _____ Be sure to use words that show how well-educated you are—the longer, the better!

b. _____ Chat with the receptionist at the office.

c. _____ Don't bother applying for a job if you don't have excellent grades.

d. _____ Mail as many resumes as you can.

e. _____ If you don't get a job offer, don't stay in touch with the company.

f. _____ Write a letter thanking the interviewer.

g. _____ Keep your job search a secret.

h. _____ If you don't know the answer to an interviewer's question, be silent.

i. _____ Don't call people to ask for interviews unless you know them.

j. _____ Call a company first to find out the name of the person you should write to.

k. _____ Try to be as formal as possible.

5. Compare your answers with a classmate's. Did you check the same ideas?

Reflect on Reading

In exercise 4, you had to **infer** meaning. When you compared your answers with your classmate's answers, you probably found that you didn't always agree. There may have been more than one correct answer. **Inferences** are often not clear-cut because they are not stated directly in the reading.

....

Targeting

Collocations Related to Work

Collocations are words that commonly go together. There is no easy way to recognize collocations. You must study them and practice using them correctly.

1. Study the collocations on the next page that relate to work.

Collocations	Examples
work/find a job as [a position]	I **worked as** a secretary for two years. I would like to **find a new job as** an office manager.
work for [an employer]	She **worked for** the insurance company for 25 years.
work with [a co-worker or client]	As a payroll consultant, he **works with** new companies to set up their payroll systems.
work/have jobs in [a field/industry]	They **work in** manufacturing. There are not many **jobs in** accounting that don't require computer knowledge.
work on [a project or specific task, a machine]	I'm **working on** vocabulary right now. The mechanic is **working on** my car. *(trying to fix)* She **works on** the computer so much that she has developed problems with her wrists. *(spends time on)*
get/find/look for [work/a job] NOTE: *Job* is a singular count noun; *work* is a noncount noun.	I started my job search three months ago, but I haven't **found** a job yet. As soon as I **get** regular work, I'm going to **look for** a new apartment.
do [work/a job/ project/program]	It's a tough job, but someone has to **do** it. They **did** the program last year and enjoyed it.
manage/direct/ run/administer [a program/ organization]	The director **runs** our department.
create/design/ set up [something]	We **set up** the program so that we wouldn't need to hire new people.
perform/carry out/ do [a job or task]	It only takes one person to **do** the job.

Collocations	Examples
earn/make [money/salary/a living] do [something] for a living	**Earning** a lot of money is not important to me. As long as they **make** enough to live on, they will be happy. What do you **do for a living**? I **make a living** painting houses.

2. *Complete the sentences with words from the collocation chart above. Use the correct form of the verb.*

I _work for_ a large company _____ a
    (a)   (b)

researcher. I used to _____ quality control and
                        (c)

new product development. However, our company president

wanted to focus on more new product development, so we

_____ a new division within our department.
        (d)

Its task was to work _____ the marketing people
                 (e)

to _____ new products.
    (f)

One problem with the new division was management. Who was

in charge of the division? Who should _____ the
                                 (g)

program? It has taken us five years to figure all this out, but now we

are all able to _____ our jobs with no problems.
                (h)

3. *On separate paper, write sentences using these words and phrases.*

a. work as	**c.** work on	**e.** a living	**g.** run
b. work for	**d.** earn	**f.** manage	

Quickwriting

WRITING TIP

If you don't know a word in English, go ahead and write it in your language. Don't stop to use the dictionary when you quickwrite!

Quickwriting helps you develop your ideas about a topic. When you **quickwrite**, write your thoughts as quickly as you can. Don't worry about details like spelling, grammar, or punctuation.

In your notebook, write for five to ten minutes about the ideal job situation for you. Try to write as quickly as possible, without stopping to edit your grammar, spelling, or ideas.

Vocabulary Log

What words or phrases would you like to remember from this chapter? Write five to ten items in your notebook. Be sure to write words that go together (prepositions, for example) and other forms of the word that you know. Also write a sentence so that you will remember how to use each new word.

Chapter 2

Getting that Job

Each company has different requirements for employees, but employment practices vary on a more global scale as well. In this chapter you will examine two resumes and cover letters and read about employment practices in different countries. Then you will write a cover letter or personal essay of your own.

Starting Point

A Hiring Decision

What makes some people better candidates for a job than others? You decide!

1. *You work in the legal department of a large corporation. One of your best legal secretaries recently retired and you are now on a committee to hire a new legal secretary. Decide in your committee what qualifications and skills you would need in a legal secretary.*

   _____   _____

   _____   _____

   _____   _____

2. *In general, which of these options make the most sense to you? Put a check (✓) beside the plan(s) of action you think your committee should follow.*

   a. _____ Hire someone who is a secretary in the company in a different part of the corporation (not the legal office).

   b. _____ Promote one of the lower-level clerical people in your office who currently files, types, and answers phones.

   c. _____ Hire someone from outside the company who has the best experience as a legal secretary.

   d. _____ Hire a relative who has secretarial experience.

Reading 1

Resumes

Which candidate would make a good legal secretary in your company?

1. *Look at the resumes of two applicants. As you read, consider which person has better qualifications for the job.*

Katerina Long
1916 Queensdown Road
Glen Burnie, MD 21230
(410) 435-6641

Career Goal   To use my strong secretarial and organizational skills in work in a legal office.

Experience

Mar. 98-present   **Executive Secretary,** Jones Air-Conditioning

Assisted the president of the company. In charge of correspondence, telephone, and filing.

Apr. 97-Mar. 98   **Administrative Assistant,** Franklin, Jones, and Alvarez Legal Offices

Promoted to clerical position handling legal documents and correspondence.

Sept. 96-Mar. 97   **Receptionist,** Franklin, Jones, and Alvarez Legal Offices

Managed Incoming calls and visitor reception.

Certificate

1996   Peterson Secretarial Course

Other

Married, no children

Enjoy downhill skiing and tennis

References available upon request

Maria Fernandez
2310 Frederick Road, Apt. 105
Catonsville, Maryland 21228
(410) 739-9264

Professional Goal

To work in a challenging and interesting environment where I can help my employer be more effective.

Legal Secretarial Experience

January 1997 to the present
McCauley, Jones, and Frasier Law Firm, **Legal Secretary**
Executive secretary to senior law partner, Jennifer Jones. Managed legal paperwork, correspondence, and appointments. Supervised two administrative assistants.

September 1991 to January 1997
Glass and Chung Legal Services, **Legal Secretary**
Managed small legal office. Responsible for legal paperwork and correspondence.

April 1987 to July 1991
Ginsberg, Wright, and Foster, **Legal Secretary**
Secretary for two attorneys. In charge of legal correspondence, appointments, and filing.

September 1985 to March 1987
Southerly Corporation, **Secretary**
Responsible for filing, typing, and telephone support.

Volunteer Experience

Present
Vice-president, Disabled Office Workers Association of Baltimore

1996
Secretary treasurer of National Association of Disabled Office Workers

Education

1987
A.D. degree in legal/secretarial skills. Catonsville Community College.

2. *Which person seems more qualified for the secretarial position in your law firm? Why? Discuss this with your classmates, who are the other members of the hiring committee.*

3. *Go back to the resumes. Underline the words or phrases the applicants chose to show that they were competent and capable employees.*

Reading 2

Hiring and Promotion in Different Cultures

This reading describes employment practices in hiring and promotion that vary from country to country.

1. *Read the following selection.*

Hiring and Promotion in Different Cultures

[1]   Employment practices vary from country to country. Some of the key differences involve recruitment, hiring, promotion, and tenure. For example, consider the careers of two executives: Monica Grant from the United States and Matsuhiro Tanaka from Japan.

[2]   Monica Grant went to a small college in Pennsylvania, which was not one of the top schools in the country. She graduated with honors and got a job in a small company in Philadelphia. After working for a few years, she went back to school. However, this time she attended the prestigious Wharton School of the University of Pennsylvania and received an M.B.A., with a specialization in finance. For the next 25 years, she worked in four different companies. With each move, she gained new responsibilities and a higher salary.

[3]   Matsuhiro Tanaka, on the other hand, earned an undergraduate degree from Keio University. With this degree, he was virtually assured of a position with a top Japanese corporation. He started as a "freshman" with a group of about six other top university graduates. Matsuhiro plans to stay with this company for the rest of his working life. He will move from one job to another within the company, rising through the ranks with his colleagues.

[4]   These examples illustrate two kinds of hiring and promotion practices. One practice is recruiting people from outside the company who have management degrees or other experience. The other is promoting from the ranks and giving raises based on seniority.

[5]   Another difference from country to country is the role of personal connections in hiring and promotion. Neither Monica nor Matsuhiro got their jobs through personal connections, but such practices are not unusual. In Latin America, for example, if you have personal connections, they say you have *palanca*. In small companies there, family and friends are often favored for jobs because they are considered more trustworthy. In other countries, promotions may be based on loyalty to a supervisor rather than on performance.

[6]   Monica's career is not unusual for a woman in the United States. In many countries, though, women are hired to fill jobs only until they leave to get married and raise children. When the economy is bad, these "temporary" workers are laid off.

[7]   Employment practices are always changing. Countries with a tradition of lifelong employment, or tenure, may have to lay people off in an economic downturn. Monica's experience of changing from company to company might not have happened in a slow growth economic period. If she had been born in a "baby boom," she might not have had as many opportunities because so many of her peers would have been trying to rise through the ranks at the same time. Luck plays a part in many careers.

2. **Take notes** *about differences in employment practices mentioned in the reading.*

education: *whether you need to get an advanced degree*

tenure: *whether you* _____

recruitment: *whether companies* _____

personal connections: *whether* _____

women in the workforce: *whether women* _____

3. *Paragraph 5 describes the practice of hiring and promoting people because of family connections or personal loyalty. In the United States, this practice is referred to as nepotism or favoritism and is considered unethical in many situations. How is it viewed among people you know in business? Discuss this question with a group of classmates.*

Reflect on Reading

Here are some typical ways to organize paragraphs and essays. Which technique(s) best describe(s) the **organization** of "Hiring and Promotion in Different Cultures"?
a. one topic with facts or examples to support it
b. steps in a process or sequence; a list of points in chronological order or in order of importance
c. emphasis on the reasons and/or the results
d. similarities and/or differences

READING TIP

If you know common endings for different **word forms,** you can improve your reading.

4. *Do you know other* **word forms** *related to these from the reading? Complete the chart below.*

From the reading	Noun, verb, adjective, or adverb	Another example
employment	noun	employ (verb)
recruitment	_____	_____
promotion	_____	_____
specialization	_____	_____
loyalty	_____	_____
supervisor	_____	_____
performance	_____	_____
virtually	_____	_____
assured	_____	_____
economy	_____	_____

ANSWER KEY

5. *Look at the words in exercise 4. What are typical endings for adjectives, nouns, adverbs, and verbs?*

Adjective ending(s):_____   Verb ending(s):_____

Noun ending(s):_____   Adverb ending(s):_____

It is important to understand how writers use transitions and repetition to connect ideas.

1. *Study these ways to connect ideas.*

Ways to Connect Ideas	*Examples*
Demonstrative adjectives or **pronouns** *(this, that)* indicate a reference to a previous word or idea as do substitution words such as *one, the other, mine, yours, some, many, such, the former,* and *the latter.*	I lost my job six years ago. **This** experience taught me a great deal. Though the classifieds listed three pages of jobs in my field, **many** were out of town.
Transition expressions show the relationships between ideas: time, sequence, comparison, contrast, cause and effect, condition, consequence, examples, conclusion, addition.	He lived in Japan for 15 years. **During that time,** he never learned to speak Japanese. (*time*) The rules vary from place to place. **Therefore,** be sure to ask what you should do. (*consequence*) The new employees thought the meeting was boring. The older workers, **on the other hand,** enjoyed the break from routine. (*contrast*)
Participial phrases also connect ideas by repeating or giving additional information.	He got a job offer in New York. **After working** for several years, he moved back to Rio.

ANSWER KEY

2. *Complete these paragraphs with words or expressions to link ideas.*

Employment practices vary from country to country.

_____ differences involve recruitment, hiring,
(a)

promotion, and tenure. _____, consider the careers
(b)

of two executives: Monica Grant from the United States and

Matsuhiro Tanaka from Japan.

Monica Grant went to a small college in Pennsylvania, which

was not one of the top schools in the country. She graduated

with honors and got a job in a small company in Philadelphia.

_____ for several years, she went back to school.
(c)

_____, this time she attended the prestigious
(d)

Wharton School of the University of Pennsylvania and received an

M.B.A., with a specialization in finance. For the next 25 years, she

worked in four different companies. With _____,
(e)

she has gained new responsibilities and a higher salary.

Matsuhiro Tanaka, _____, had an under-
(f)

graduate degree from Keio, a top university in Japan. With

_____, he was virtually assured a position with a
(g)

top Japanese corporation. He started as a "freshman" with a group of

about six other top university graduates. Matsuhiro plans to stay with

_____ company for the rest of his working life.
(h)

He will move from one job to another within the company, rising

through the ranks with his colleagues.

_____ illustrate different types of hiring and
(i)

promotion practices. _____ is recruiting people from
(j)

outside the company who have management degrees or other

experience. _____ is promoting from the ranks and
(k)

giving raises based on seniority.

_____ common practice in some countries is hir-
(l)

ing and promoting through personal connections. Neither Monica

nor Matsuhiro got their jobs in this way, but _____
(m)

practices are not unusual. In Latin America, _____, if
(n)

you have lots of connections, they say you have *palanca*. In areas

where there are a lot of small companies, family and friends are often

favored for jobs because they are considered more trustworthy.

_____, promotions may also be based on loyalty to a
(o)

supervisor rather than on performance.

Monica's career is not unusual for a woman in the United States.

In many countries, _____, women are hired to fill jobs
(p)

with the idea that they will leave within a few years to get married

and raise children. When the economy is bad, _____
(q)

"temporary" workers are laid off.

Writing

Preparing to Write 1: Analyzing the Style and Format of Formal Letters

The two applicants for the legal secretary position described in Starting Point on pages 10–11 wrote cover letters for their resumes. Cover letters are one kind of formal letter.

1. *Identify these elements in each cover letter. Write the letters of the elements in the circles.*

   a. opening statement: the reason for writing

   b. name and address of recipient

   c. salutation

   d. written signature

   e. closing statement

   f. printed name

   g. name and address of sender

   h. closing phrase

   i. date

   j. main message

Katerina Long
1916 Queensdown Road
Glen Burnie, MD 21230
(410) 435-6641 ◯

October 5, XXXX ◯

Personnel Director
Clark, Liu, and Jones Legal Offices
101 Calvert Street, Suite 1900
Baltimore, MD 21228 ◯

Dear Personnel Director: ◯

I am writing in response to your ad for a legal secretary. ◯

As a highly skilled legal secretary with experience in a variety of office settings, I am confident that I would make an excellent secretary in your law office. ◯

As you can see from the enclosed resume, I have experience working in a large legal firm and in a small company where I was an executive secretary. In these positions, I have learned to take care of a variety of tasks.

I also get along well with people and am an effective communicator.

I look forward to hearing from you about scheduling an ◯ appointment at your earliest convenience.

Sincerely yours, ◯

Katerina Long ◯
Katerina Long ◯

Maria Fernandez
2310 Frederick Road, Apt. 105
Cantonsville, MD 21228
(410) 739-9264

October 3, XXXX

Tom Liu, Senior Partner
Clark, Liu, and Jones Legal Offices
101 Calvert Street, Suite 1900
Baltimore, MD 21228

Dear Mr. Liu:

Francine Jeffers suggested that I contact you about the opening in your firm for a new legal secretary. I know it must be difficult to replace a secretary you have worked with for so many years, but Francine thought that I might have the qualities that you are looking for.

As you can see from my resume, I have almost 15 years of experience as a legal secretary. I have worked in a variety of situations, from being a secretary for two attorneys at once to being a secretary for a senior law partner with two people assisting me.

I have enjoyed the work in all these offices. A good legal secretary is essential to a good lawyer, and I have enjoyed helping the attorneys do their jobs well. I am looking for a new position now because Ms. Jones is going to retire this month. Although I could get another job in this office, I think that it would be more interesting to go to a new firm if I can find one that is a good match for me.

I would appreciate having the opportunity to talk with you about my experience and the specific needs in your office. Thank you.

Sincerely,

Maria Fernandez

Maria Fernandez

2. *Discuss these questions with your classmates.*

    a. In your opinion, which letter writer is more likely to get a job interview? Why?

    b. Consider the content and style of the letters. How does each writer try to convince the reader that she would be a good choice for the job?

Preparing to Write 2: Planning

Planning what you want to say will help make your writing more focused and easier to understand.

1. *In a job cover letter or an essay for a program application, how could you convince the reader that you would be a good choice? Write your notes here.*

   Job/Program you are applying for: _____

   Your strengths: _____

   _____

   _____

   A possible opening sentence for your letter or essay:

   _____

   A possible closing statement:

   _____

Writing a Formal Letter or Personal Essay

Complete one of these writing assignments.

1. Write a formal cover letter to enclose a resume.

2. Write an essay for an application for admission to a program in a college or university.

3. Write a formal letter to request information.

> A formal letter follows business letter format. For examples of **business letter format**, see pages 205–206 in Reference.

Editing and Rewriting

....

Editing for Verb Tense Errors

Always reread your writing to check for correct use of verb tenses. Look for time clues that show the need for the past or the future tense.

1. *Study the rules on the next page.*

Rules	Examples
Use the present tense for habits, facts, and general truths.	Job stability **depends** on many factors. Workers in the medical profession generally **have** higher salaries.
Be careful with subject/verb agreement in the present tense. Check for singular subjects. Don't forget to add the final -s (or -es) to the verb that follows a third person singular subject.	Each of the workers **contributes** to the success or failure of a company. He **goes** to work at 5:30 A.M. every day.
Use the simple past tense for facts and events that happened in the past.	I **got** my first job at age 16. When she was in college, she **didn't know** what she wanted to do.
Use the present perfect for facts and events that happened in the past, are continuing now, or may happen again.	I **have** always **loved** my job. Our company **has hired** a lot of people with disabilities.
Use the simple future (**will** + verb) or (**be going to** + verb) to talk about events in the future.	I **am going to look** for a job as soon as I graduate. She's the director's niece, so he **will** never **fire** her.
Modal auxiliary verbs give information about the writer's perception, attitude, or intention. Be careful to use the base form after these verbs.	In a job search, you **should** try to make as many contacts as possible. (*opinion*) My brother has been looking for a job for a year. He **must** feel very frustrated. (*probability, necessity*)
Modals such as **would** and **could** act as "distancers" to make a statement more polite.	I **would** appreciate any help you **could** give me.

For more information about past tense verbs, see page 210 in Reference.

2. *Correct the verb tense errors in the following sentences. Not all sentences have mistakes.*

a. Sue Evans suggested that I send you my resume. One of my

dreams ~~are~~ *is* to work in a hotel. I looking for a job that will be

challenging and rewarding and I am confident that I contribute

a great deal to your organization. I would appreciate having the

opportunity to speak with you about my qualifications and

interest in your company.

b. I graduated from Holgate University and major in American

literature. Now I look for a job in education. I want to teach

children whose parents was born in different countries.

c. I like to work in international business and I have always wanted

to work for a company such as yours. I have had a great deal of

experience in computer programming when I was an intern in

the Regents Company. There I assisted Robert Learner on several

programming projects. Each of these projects have offered me

opportunities to learn new skills.

d. Please let me know what this job is requiring. I would like to start

work as soon as I will graduate. I hope you call me for an inter-

view as soon as possible. I looking forward to hearing from you.

e. In my last job I have been responsible for many clerical tasks. My

responsibilities were including filing, answering phones, and

EDITING TIP

Look for time clues *(always, today, last year, recently)* to help you determine the verb tense.

typing. None of my jobs have offered this level of responsibility, but I feel that I am capable of doing more. I will appreciate your considering me for this job.

Editing Checklist

Check the Content

1. *Exchange your writing with a classmate. After you read your classmate's work, answer these questions:*

   ❑ Imagine that you are considering your classmate for a job or program. Is it clear why he or she is well qualified?

   ❑ Did the writer include sufficient information about his or her qualifications and interest in the program or job?

Check the Details

2. *Read your own writing again. If necessary, revise. Add or change details. Then continue checking your work. Use these questions:*

   ❑ Is the format clear and consistent?

   ❑ Check your letter with the list of elements in a formal letter in Preparing to Write on page 18. Did you include all these elements?

   ❑ Check your verb forms for correct subject-verb agreement and tense.

3. *Revise your writing.*

Vocabulary Log

What words or phrases would you like to remember from this chapter? Write five to ten items in your notebook.

Grammar and Punctuation Review

Look over your writing from this chapter. What changes did you need to make in grammar and punctuation? Write them in your notebook. Review them before the next writing assignment.

Chapter 3

Reasonable Accommo-dations

Imagine how difficult a job search can be for someone with disabilities. In this chapter you will read about government legislation to help people with disabilities. Then you will consider the accessibility of a place near you and write a survey report.

Starting Point

Challenges in the Workplace

When you are disabled, you face special difficulties on the job.

1. *If Maria Fernandez, pictured below, worked at your program, what challenges might she find there? Discuss these questions with a classmate.*

   a. What jobs would be easy or difficult for her? Why?

   b. What physical elements (stairs, doorways) in the setting would be challenging for her?

   c. Do you think employers need to be responsible for making the workplace accessible to people with disabilities?

People with disabilities in the United States were successful in persuading their government to force companies to make changes to accommodate them.

1. *Read the selection below to **identify the topic** of each section. Write the appropriate headings in the blanks in the selection.*

Employment   Public Services   Telecommunications

Miscellaneous   Public Accommodations

Accommodations for Disabilities

In 1990, the United States government passed the Americans with Disabilities Act (ADA). The ADA is a group of laws affecting many aspects of American life, including work and public services. The purpose of the ADA is to make American society more open to people with disabilities.

It is divided into five titles (sections of legislation):

- Title I _____
  Businesses with more than 15 employees must provide "reasonable accommodations" to protect the rights of people with disabilities. These changes may include restructuring jobs, altering the layout of work areas, or modifying equipment. Companies may also have to change their application process, hiring, wages, and benefits to make sure that disabled people have the same access to jobs as able-bodied people.

- Title II _____
  Public services cannot deny services to people with disabilities. Public services include state and local governments and national transportation or commuter services. Any program that is available to people without disabilities must also be available to those who are disabled. In addition, public transportation systems, such as public transit buses, must be accessible to people with disabilities.

- Title III _____
  All new buildings or additions to old buildings must provide access to people with disabilities. For existing buildings, any barriers to services must be removed, if possible. Public accommodations include facilities such as restaurants, hotels, grocery stores, and retail stores as well as privately owned transportation systems. It does not matter how many people are employed in the facility.

- Title IV _____
  Companies that offer telephone service to the general public must have special services for deaf people.

- Title V _____
  This title prohibits people from threatening or taking action against the disabled or those who try to help the disabled get their rights under the ADA.

ANSWER KEY

2. *Complete the sentences below with these words from "Accommodations for Disabilities." Be careful to use the correct form of any verbs.*

accessible	disabilities	protect
alter	disabled	reasonable
available	modify	restructure
deny	prohibit	right

   a. The legislation _____ anyone from threatening

      people trying to force companies to follow the ADA laws.

   b. The company has to make _____ accommoda-

      tions for people with _____.

   c. Bus service was _____, but it wasn't

      _____ because someone in a wheelchair could

      not get on the bus.

   d. You cannot _____ access to someone with a dis-

      ability. You must allow everyone to come in.

   e. It is fairly easy to _____ an office to accommo-

      date a wheelchair. It is more difficult to _____ a

      job because more people are affected by the changes.

   f. This legislation _____ the rights of the

      _____.

   g. I have a legal _____ to vote in the election.

3. *Discuss these questions with your classmates.*

   a. What are the effects of the ADA laws? Consider the impacts on businesses and also on individuals with disabilities.

b. How do these laws compare to the situation in other countries you are familiar with?

4. *In chapter 2 you examined word forms. Analyzing **word forms** and understanding how words are used in sentences are important reading skills. How are the **boldface** words used in the sentences below? Write adjective, noun, verb, or adverb on the line.*

Businesses must provide **reasonable**
(1)

1. _____

accommodations to protect the rights
(2)

2. _____

of individuals with **disabilities** in all
(3)

3. _____

aspects of **employment**.
(4)

4. _____

Employment aspects may include the
(5)

5. _____

application process, hiring, wages,
(6)

6. _____

and benefits.

A **disabled** person may not be able to
(7)

7. _____

access the workplace.
(8)

8. _____

Building a ramp for a wheelchair is one

9. _____

example of how a business can

10. _____

accommodate the needs of the **disabled**.
(9)   (10)

For **existing** facilities, barriers to services
(11)

11. _____

must be removed.

Reading 2

Know Your Rights—and Go for the Job!

What does the ADA mean to disabled applicants and their potential employers?

1. *How does the Americans with Disabilities Act ("Accommodations for Disabilities," page 25) affect common situations in business? Do you think the following situations would be legal or illegal according to the ADA? Write "legal" or "illegal" on the line.*

   a. _____ A bank requires all new employees to pass a general medical exam.

   b. _____ An airline requires pilots to pass a medical exam stating that they do not have a heart condition.

   c. _____ A child care center refused to hire a deaf person to be the only caregiver in one class.

   d. _____ A company requires all new employees to show their drivers' licenses for identification.

   e. _____ A store does not allow guide dogs to come inside.

   f. _____ A three-story hotel has no elevator.

   g. _____ A three-story house with an apartment for rent on the top floor has no elevator.

   h. _____ A desk is too low to accommodate a wheelchair, so a company refuses to hire someone who uses a wheelchair.

i. _____ A school refuses to hire someone in a wheelchair to teach physical education.

j. _____ A company allows most of its employees to take a break every three hours, but allows a disabled person to take a break every hour.

2. ***Preview*** *the reading. First, consider the title. Then* ***skim*** *the reading. Decide what kind of organizational style the writer uses. Here are some possibilities: steps in a process or sequence; a list of points in chronological order or in order of importance; or one topic with facts or examples.*

3. *Now read the selection.*

Know Your Rights—and Go for the Job!

[1]   Barbara Bernhart, Florida's director of the Coordinating Council on the Americans with Disabilities Act, says even though the disabled do have more difficulty finding work, they should not give up. If they know their legal rights and their accommodation needs, they will be more successful.

[2]   "On a job interview, for example, do not bring up a discussion of your disability, even when it's visible. When you do that, you're opening the door to eliminating one of your rights. You may not want to discuss your disability at all; it may be very private. You don't have to. Discuss only how you can do this job. Under the ADA, it's now illegal for the potential employer to ask you any health question either on your application or in an interview." An employer may, however, ask a disabled applicant about the ability to perform specific job functions. Within limitations, he or she may also ask that person how those functions can be met with that particular disability.

[3]   Under the Americans with Disabilities Act (ADA), any public or private business with a staff of 15 or more people is now required by law to be accessible. Reasonable accommodation must be provided to the disabled. A company, however, does not have to provide that access if the changes would cause a financial hardship. They are also exempt from ADA when the changes would alter the business's original intent.

ANSWER KEY

READING TIP

Previewing a reading by **skimming** helps you understand a difficult reading. When you skim, look at the text quickly and find the general idea. Look at the first sentences of paragraphs. Don't worry about reading individual words or understanding details at this point.

[4]   Consider, for example, that you are a recently graduated chef who uses a wheelchair. You apply for a job at a well-known restaurant where the entire kitchen has already been set up. For the owner to redo the kitchen completely would be considered a hardship. Bernhart says this would be an unreasonable accommodation, and changes would not have to be made. Still, she says, don't give up.

[5]   "At the time of the interview, the disabled applicant has no idea about the owner's financial situation. Don't assume that employer wouldn't be willing to accommodate. He might be looking for a write-off or a loss." Employers are allowed to take a federal tax credit to make accommodations for the disabled. That credit, she adds, can go as high as $15,000 a year when major architectural barriers and complete renovations are involved.

[6]   Bernhart has an excellent, real-life example. A well-known Central Florida surf and beach shop recently put in a whole range of disabled accommodations to make sure all employees could get around the public store easily. After the changes were made, she says, the owner pleasantly discovered accessibility meant a fantastic savings of both time and money to his company.

[7]   "Suddenly everybody could use the elevator to get things up to the second floor. It was no longer a big thing to get from one place to another. The owner could not only display his things faster, but that, of course, meant he could sell them faster, too. Again, when you're in an interview situation, you just never know what's going on behind the scenes. This owner had a disabled mother, and he wanted his mom to be able to come inside his store. He made more than the necessary changes. So don't assume—ever."

[8]   Bernhart gives another employment situation involving intent. "Let's say you're a cocktail waitress who has a visual impairment and you're applying for a job in a new town. You notice in the lounge the lights are dim and you have trouble seeing. You didn't have that before. Could you ask the owner to turn up the lights? No, that would probably ruin the atmosphere the owner's worked so hard to create, would alter the nature of the business, another unreasonable accommodation. But could you, say, ask that employer to give you a small flashlight to help take orders? Yes. That's reasonable accommodation."

[9]   "It doesn't always mean knocking out a whole wall to put in a heavy-duty elevator," she explains. "There are stairgliders that can work, closet

elevators. Employers shouldn't immediately panic. There are a lot of products out there now and employers and disabled job seekers owe it to themselves to investigate them and know where they can be found." It is helpful, Bernhart says, for a disabled candidate to know before the interview starts what he may need for his particular situation. Businesses think it will cost thousands of dollars, but Bernhart has found that most accommodations cost less than $50. The actual providing of reasonable accommodations on the job falls upon the employer. It does not fall upon the disabled looking for work.

[10]   Bernhart says in the backs of their minds, many disabled are still afraid when they go to an interview. In no way does the ADA force an employer to hire the disabled, and for all the new changes in the law, it still can come down to which applicant that employer wants to hire, which applicant he or she feels has the best qualifications. But when you know what your rights are, it's a little easier.

4. *Go back to exercise 1. **Apply the information** from the reading and check to see if you still have the same opinion about whether the situations listed are legal or illegal.*

5. *Look at this list of words. Which **category** are the words related to—(1) business, (2) building, or (3) law? Write **1, 2,** or **3** on the lines.*

  a. __1__ job functions   **f.** _____ rights

  b. _____ architectural   **g.** _____ renovations

  c. _____ write-off or a loss   **h.** _____ tax credit

  d. _____ barriers   **i.** _____ legal

  e. _____ financial hardship

6. *Read each pair of sentences. Which sentence in each pair is specific? Which is general? Write **S** or **G** on the lines.*

  a. __S__ Under the ADA, it's now illegal for the potential employer to ask you any health question.

      __G__ If they know their legal rights and their accommodation needs, they will be more successful.

  b. _____ For the owner to redo the kitchen completely would be considered a hardship.

      _____ A company does not have to provide access if the changes would cause a financial hardship.

READING TIP

Being able to distinguish between the **main idea** and **specific details** is an important reading skill. The main idea is usually the most general idea. Specific details support the main idea. When you look for the main idea, decide which ideas are specific and which are more general.

c. _____ Reasonable accommodation must be provided to the disabled.

_____ Could you ask an employer to give you a small flashlight?

d. _____ Companies are also exempt from ADA when the changes would alter the business's original intent.

_____ Could you ask the owner to turn up the lights? No, that would probably ruin the atmosphere the owner's worked so hard to create.

e. _____ Under the Americans with Disabilities Act (ADA), any business or governmental organization with a staff of 15 or more people is now required by law to be accessible.

_____ A company, however, does not have to provide that access if the changes would cause a financial hardship.

7. *A friend of yours with a physical disability has just graduated from college and is about to start looking for a job in the United States. Write a letter to your friend* **summarizing** *the information you learned in this chapter. Use separate paper.*

Writing

Preparing to Write 1: Survey

How easy or difficult is it for people with disabilities to work or live near you? In this section, you will make a report on a survey.

1. *With a partner, choose a place near your classroom where people work; for example, your building, a hotel, library, grocery store, or office. Go to that place.*

2. *Take notes about this place. Here are some things to think about.*

- Consider the structure of the place. Can people with disabilities get in and around? List examples of what you see.

- Consider the jobs you see people doing. Could someone with a disability do the job? What accommodations might need to be made?

- Consider the services the place provides. Would the organization need to change any of the services or the ways they are provided in order to make them available to everyone, including people with disabilities?

Once you have some information about your topic, you need to decide what information to include and how to organize it.

1. *With your partner, look at your notes from your survey. How could you organize the information in a report? Which information will you need a list for? A chart?*

2. *Write an introduction to your report.*

3. *Prepare any lists or charts that you plan to use. Be careful to write the information in a consistent form. Be sure that each chart or list is connected to the report with an introductory sentence (this may be the introduction to your report).*

4. *Does your report need a conclusion? In many situations, reports include suggestions for action.*

Make a report on your survey.

∙∙∙

One of the biggest problems with charts and lists is presenting the information in a consistent form. Each element in the chart or list needs to have the same structure and format.

1. *Study the information on page 34 about being consistent in charts.*

Preparing to Write 2: Planning

WRITING TIP

Remember that too much detail can make a chart difficult to read. If you use any symbols, abbreviations, or colors in your chart, consider using a "legend" or key to explain them.

Writing a Survey Report

Editing and Rewriting

Editing for Consistency in Charts and Lists

Elements to check for consistency	Examples
structure	They need to **review** their policies, **discuss** their options, and **make** any necessary changes. *(base form of verbs)* The important areas to consider are the following: • **making** physical changes to allow better access • **changing** recruiting and interviewing procedures • **reviewing** company policies *(gerunds)*
format	Examples of workplace accommodations

Physical Structure	**Interviews**	**Policies**
• higher desks • wider doors	• focus on abilities • no questions about disability	• change in medical exam requirement • review of seniority policy

punctuation and capitalization	Accommodations needed
	   Hiring: interviews and recruitment
	   Office: physical changes
	   Policies: seniority and medical leave

2. *Correct the problems with consistency in the following lists and charts.*

   a. These simple changes can help your company

     • maintain better morale

     • improvement of employee relations

     • follow the law

b. To make accommodations for a secretary with hearing loss, be sure to write notes from office meetings, add hearing devices to the telephone, and checking with the National Association for the Hearing Impaired.

c.

Situation	Old Approach	New Approach
Old building with limited access	do nothing	build better access

d. To comply with the law,

- some changes in interview questions
- review employment policies
- survey the work site

e. There are three steps to the process:

1) Analyze your employment policies and standard procedures.
2) Survey the work site to determine accessibility.
3) Study of the products and services your organization provides.

Editing Checklist

Check the Content

1. *Exchange your survey report with a classmate. After you read your classmate's work, answer these questions:*

   ❏ Are the parts of the survey report clearly organized?
   ❏ Are charts and lists clear and easy to read?
   ❏ Can you understand what changes need to be made in the workplace?

Check the Details

2. *Read your own report again. If necessary, revise. Add or change details. Then continue checking your paper. Use these questions:*

   ❏ Are all charts or lists clear and consistent? Check for format, capitalization, punctuation, and grammar.
   ❏ Does every list or chart have an explanation or clear connection to the report?
   ❏ Check your verb forms for correct subject-verb agreement and tense.

3. *Revise your writing.*

Vocabulary Log

What words or phrases would you like to remember from this chapter? Write five to ten items in your notebook.

Grammar and Punctuation Review

Look over your writing from this chapter. What changes did you need to make in grammar and punctuation? Write them in your notebook. Review them before the next writing assignment.

Class Activity

Work in a group. Choose one of these activities. Report back to the class on what you learn.

1 Go to a medical equipment store. What products help people with disabilities? Is the technology new or old?

2 Think of as many job or career possibilities as you can that are related to working with people with disabilities. Find out more information about these jobs.

3 Ask to interview someone with a disability.

2 The Living Language

Nothing is more important than the way people communicate with each other. However, sometimes the way people use language makes it difficult to communicate clearly. These are some of the activities you will do in this unit:

- Read about strategies for successful conflict resolution
- Read about a situation in which speaking one's native language is an issue
- Read about whether English-only policies are legal
- Study vocabulary to express demands
- Write a response to an English-only policy announcement
- Read about differences in the ways that men and women communicate
- Study vocabulary to use when reporting on point of view
- Write a summary

Chapter 4

It's Not *What* You Say—It's *How*

In many situations, at home, at work, or at school, people have disagreements. In this chapter you will read about strategies for resolving these disagreements and practice applying the suggestions in the reading.

Starting Point

The Power of Words

Tone and choice of words can make a huge difference in the way that a reader or listener responds to what someone says.

1. *Discuss the following letters and conversations with a classmate. What is the difference in the tone between the ones in column A and the ones in column B?*

A	B
You sent a defective computer desk assembly kit to me. It is missing part 101 and part 265. I can't believe the poor quality control that your company has. This is inexcusable! If anyone else made this kit, I would demand my money back. You had better send me the missing parts immediately or I will report your company to the Better Business Bureau.	I recently ordered your computer desk assembly kit. Unfortunately, it is missing two pieces, part 101 and part 265. Please send these replacement parts immediately to my address above. I would also appreciate receiving some compensation for the time I have spent trying to work around the poor service I have received from your organization. Thank you.
"Why are you doing it that way? That's not the right way to do it!"	"How's it going? Is it hard to do it that way?"

2. *What word choices make a difference here? How is the general approach of each different?*

3. *Which approach do you think would be more effective? Why?*

· ·

This selection outlines strategies for resolving conflicts and disagreements.

1. *Read the following selection.*

"Win-Win" Strategies

[1]   In the early 1980s, Roger Fisher and William Ury wrote a best-selling book called *Getting to Yes: Negotiating Agreement Without Giving In*. The theories in *Getting to Yes* have become the basis for a ream of other advice about how to resolve conflicts and negotiate successfully.

[2]   Fisher and Ury's basic premise is that the adversarial model of conflict resolution, in which one side "wins" while the other "loses," is not effective in many cases. They proposed a "win-win" model whereby each party shares common goals and cooperates in order to solve the problem.

[3]   Fisher, Ury, and other experts in negotiating recommend the following strategies in order to create a win-win environment. First, listen actively to the other person. Use statements such as "I understand how you feel" and "I can see that you're upset" to acknowledge the other person's concerns and feelings. Also, clarify and restate what the other person is saying to make sure that you understand the other person's views. Say, "You think that . . ." or "Do you mean . . . ?" If you try to focus on getting the basic information in the open instead of making a judgment or expressing any opinion at this stage, you will defuse the other person's anger and reassure him or her that you are sincere about reaching an agreement.

[4]   After finding out the other person's point of view, try to agree before you disagree. Sandwich your negative ideas in positive statements. Focus on objectives that you both share. In giving your perspective on the situation, try to be objective by avoiding judgmental, "loaded" language. Don't focus on or criticize the other person's actions. Instead, talk about your own perspective and feelings by using "I" statements instead of "you" statements. Try to keep your tone of voice unemotional and, if possible, use more indirect ways to express demands. For example, say, "I would appreciate knowing . . ." instead of "Tell me . . ." Make small

concessions to show that you are willing to cooperate and, above all, keep the focus on working collaboratively to try to solve the problem.

[5] This type of collaborative approach may not be appropriate in every situation. In negotiating the best price for a car, for example, there is clearly a winner and a loser, no matter how polite the negotiations. However, in many cases, taking this collaborative approach to resolving differences works effectively. It's worth a try, at any rate. You can always go back to yelling and screaming if this doesn't work!

2. **Analyze the reading** by answering these questions.

   a. In which paragraph(s) does the author of this selection

      1. _____ develop her main point

      2. _____ summarize Fisher and Ury's ideas

      3. _____ introduce the topic

      4. _____ conclude

   b. Why did the author write this article?

      1. _____ to talk about Fisher and Ury, the authors of a book called *Getting to Yes: Negotiating Agreement Without Giving In*

      2. _____ to summarize different points of view

      3. _____ to talk about strategies for resolving conflicts

   c. What style(s) of organization does the author use?

      1. _____ Chronological order

      2. _____ Examples

      3. _____ Listing steps in a process

      4. _____ Comparison and contrast

      5. _____ Cause and effect

   d. What transitional words and expressions in the reading show this organization clearly? _____

   e. Do you agree with the author's main ideas? Why or why not? _____

_____

_____

3. *Find words in the reading selection with the same meaning as these words.*

   a. [1] large number/amount   _____

   b. [1] settle   _____

   c. [1] disagreements   _____

   d. [2] idea   _____

   e. [2] opposing   _____

   f. [2] works together   _____

   g. [3] approaches to solving a problem   _____

   h. [3] ask questions to understand better   _____

   i. [4] goals you are working toward   _____

   j. [4] unbiased, expressing no opinion   _____

   k. [4] loaded   _____

   l. [4] say negative things about   _____

   m. [4] point of view   _____

   n. [4] something you give in on   _____

4. *If you know common endings for different **word forms**, you can improve your reading. Do you know other word forms related to these from the reading?*

From the reading	Noun, verb, adjective, or adverb	Another form
theories	*noun*	*theorize (verb)* *theoretical (adj.)*
negotiate	_____	_____ _____

From the reading	Noun, verb, adjective, or adverb	Another form
adversarial	_____	_____
resolution	_____	_____
effective	_____	_____
clarify	_____	_____
statements	_____	_____
		_____
acknowledge	_____	_____
concessions	_____	_____
collaboratively	_____	_____
	_____	_____

5. *What are the techniques that the authors suggest for creating a win-win situation? Then compare your list with a classmate's list.*

_____

_____

_____

_____

_____

6. *Read the following letter of complaint written to the director of an athletic facility at a college.* **Apply information** *from the reading. How does the writer <u>not</u> follow the approach suggested in the reading?*

Trent Jackson
1430 130th St. N.W.
Seattle, WA 98101

April 2, XXXX

Anna Varga
Director of Athletics
West College
1850 N.W. 120th
Seattle, WA 98101

Dear Ms. Varga:

I am writing to you because this athletic
program is unbelievably bad. I can't believe
the facilities or the crummy instructors you
have for your courses. I can play tennis
better than they can!

I paid a lot of money to come here, so the
sports facilities and programs shouldn't be
this bad. You need new equipment, better
trained instructors, and more courses to
choose from. Also, the hours are terrible.
The building should be open later at night.

I would like to talk to you in person about
this, but you are never in your office when
I come by. I'll come by again on Friday
afternoon.

Sincerely,

Trent Jackson

Trent Jackson

7. *Change the following statements from the letter in exercise 6 to be less adversarial. Once again, **apply information** from the reading. You may want to take out a sentence completely. Also, consider the appropriate tone for a formal letter. Compare your answers to a classmate's.*

a. I am writing to you because this athletic program is unbelievably

bad. _____

_____

_____

b. I can't believe the facilities or the crummy instructors you have

for your courses. _____

_____

_____

c. I can play tennis better than they can. _____

_____

_____

d. I paid a lot of money to come here, so the sports facilities and

programs shouldn't be this bad. _____

_____

_____

e. You need new equipment, better trained instructors, and more

courses to choose from. _____

_____

_____

f. Also, the hours are terrible. The building should be open later at

night. _____

_____

_____

g. I would like to talk to you in person about this, but you are never

in your office when I come by. I'll come by again on Friday after-

noon. _____

_____

_____

Do you notice a difference in how direct or indirect people are in different cultures? How effective are you at getting people to say yes? In your notebook, write for five to ten minutes on one of these topics.

Quickwriting

Chapter 5

A Word to the Wise

In many homes and workplaces, people speak different languages, and this sometimes causes problems. In this chapter you will read questions to a newspaper advice columnist and to a lawyer about some of these issues. Then you will write a response to a company policy.

Starting Point

What's Your Opinion?

Sometimes having family and coworkers with different languages is challenging.

1. Work with a partner or a small group. As you read each situation, answer these questions:

   • What is each person's point of view?

   • Why does each person feel the way he or she does?

   • What are possible solutions in this situation?

   a. Zerina and Mike have two young children. Zerina speaks her native Bosnian language to them, but Mike wants the children to speak only English at home.

   b. There are six employees in a work team at a manufacturing company. Four people are native Spanish speakers. They usually speak to each other in Spanish. The other two employees don't understand Spanish.

   c. In a large hospital, the employees are from a lot of different countries. In the cafeteria, the manager is thinking about implementing an English-only policy.

   d. A manager has two excellent employees and an opportunity to promote one of them. He chose Katherine for the promotion instead of Yuri because Katherine is easier for everyone to understand. Yuri speaks English as a second language.

   Do you think the manager's decision in item d is legal in the United States, or does it discriminate on the basis of national origin?

When someone doesn't understand the language that other people are speaking, he or she feels excluded. One woman wrote to a newspaper columnist to ask for advice about this situation.

1. *Read this letter to newspaper columnist "Dear Abby."*

> **DEAR ABBY:** My husband, "Yuri," came here from Russia six years ago. We have been married five years. Yuri speaks excellent English. He has mentioned several times that it would be a good idea for me to learn Russian, but with two small children under 4, learning Russian has not been a high priority for me.
>
> The problem is that Yuri has many Russian friends, mostly professional people who speak English very well. But when they come to visit, they speak Russian, and I am left out.
>
> Last Sunday, "Natasha" came over. I served cookies and coffee and tried to be a good hostess. She directed all her conversation to Yuri. When I asked her about her children and her job, she gave me brief answers in English, then turned to Yuri and continued speaking to him in Russian.
>
> I realize she's Yuri's friend. I'm not jealous of her, nor do I suspect they are having an affair. I just think it's very rude of her to ignore me when she's here.
>
> Abby, it's not only Natasha. It has gotten to the point that when his Russian friends come over, I go to our bedroom and watch TV.
>
> It's the same when we go to Natasha's house — or Sergei's or Ilona's. Their husbands and wives all speak Russian, and I'm left to play with the children. When I tell Yuri how I feel, he says it is much easier for them to express themselves in Russian than in English.
>
> I have decided to learn more Russian, but what do I do in the meantime? Should I insist they speak English so I can understand them — or what?
> – Fed up in Canada

2. *Analyze the selection. What are the basic issues in this situation?*

_____

3. *What do you think is the best solution to the problem?*

_____

ANSWER KEY

4. *Now read Abby's response. Do you agree or disagree?*

> **DEAR FED UP:** Ask Yuri to compromise; suggest that he ask his friends to speak English part of the time they spend with you, while you learn the language.
>
> A crash course in Russian would be a good beginning in overcoming the language barrier. Also ask Yuri to teach you a few phrases every day. You'll be amazed at how quickly you can join in their conversation.

(ANSWER KEY)

5. *Complete these sentences with the best choice of the words in parentheses.*

a. They reached a _____ in their disagreement about language. (barrier, compromise)

b. I don't know how to _____ this problem. (compromise, overcome)

c. Communicating effectively has a high _____ in any relationship. (expression, priority)

d. What is _____ to do when no one pays any attention to me? (left, the point)

e. This situation has reached the _____ where they need help. (point, priority)

f. They didn't have much time to learn the language, so they took a _____ course in Spanish. (communication, crash)

g. I don't want to _____ that they change, but asking politely doesn't seem to help. (insist, mention)

h. If they talk about it, they will be able to _____ their problems. (direct, overcome)

Quickwriting

Your Opinion

Have you ever experienced a situation similar to the one in the letter to "Dear Abby"? In your notebook, write for five to ten minutes about your experience.

. . . .

Having more than one language at home can cause friction, but it can also be a source of problems in the workplace.

1. *The selection below is taken from a Web site with frequently asked questions (FAQs) about employment issues. First, read the question only.* **Analyze** *the question. What is the basic problem in this person's work site?*

_____

2. *Can you* **predict** *what the answer will be? Based on your own knowledge, what are some possible solutions to this problem?*

_____

3. *Now read the lawyer's answer.*

Frequently Asked Questions

Q. *How should an employer handle a situation where all employees speak English, but two employees insist on speaking to each other in another language and their co-workers complain about it?*

A. Implementing language restrictions in the workplace isn't necessarily illegal. It depends on how restrictive the rule is and your reasons for implementing it. An English-only or similar rule could be seen by a court as discriminatory. Here are two cases, involving English-only rules, which you may be interested in reading before implementing language restrictions of your own.

A bank ordered four Hispanic employees to speak English at all times unless speaking Spanish was necessary to complete bank business or the employees were helping Spanish-speaking customers. The bank had received numerous complaints from non-Spanish-speaking co-workers. They complained that a hostile environment was created when the Hispanic employees talked about them and made fun of them in Spanish.

The four employees sued the bank. They claimed that an English-only rule discriminated against them because of their national origin and race. A district court disagreed. Reasons: The law does not protect an employee's right to speak his/her native tongue on the job. Just as swearing may be prohibited from the workplace, "speaking one's native tongue at any time on the job is not a privilege of employment."[1] And in this case, the bank implemented the rule to reduce friction among employees.

In another case, however, a store was ordered to change its English-only policy. They were allowed to require English only when employees were "dealing directly with a customer."[2]

Before implementing an English-only rule, play the part of the devil's advocate before you get burned in court. Consider these factors.

1. *Examine carefully the reasons why you want to implement such a rule. Does it solve or fulfill a legitimate business need?*

2. *Look at how broad-reaching the rule is. Is it unduly restrictive to employees?*

3. *Consider potential effects of the rule. Could it ultimately cause more harm than good? Some courts consider English-only rules discriminatory if the employee can't speak English and is put at a disadvantage in the workplace.*

[1] (Long v. First Union Corp. of Virginia, E.D.VA, 68 FEP Cases 917, 1996)
[2] (Kim v. the Southland Corp., Arlington HRC, Nos. 93-161-E and 93-195-E, 1995)

4. *Find words in the reading with the same meaning as these words.*

a. [1] deal with _____	**h.** [4] said strongly _____
b. [1] feel very strongly about _____	**i.** [4] using bad language _____
c. [2] putting into effect _____	**j.** [4] forbidden _____
d. [2] rules that limit _____	**k.** [4] a special right or benefit _____
e. [2] treating people differently because of differences in national origin, race, or gender _____	**l.** [4] disagreement _____
	m. [6] real _____
	n. [6] wide _____
	o. [6] unnecessarily _____
f. [3] hateful and angry _____	**p.** [6] possible _____
g. [4] took legal action, took someone to court _____	**q.** [6] in the end _____

5. *Answer the following questions.*

a. What, if anything, is similar about the topics of Reading 1 and Reading 2?

_____

b. Why is speaking a different language (from what others are speaking) at home or at work an issue?

_____

c. According to "Frequently Asked Questions" (FAQs), which issue is most important to a court deciding whether an English-only policy is legal or illegal?

1. whether the rule discriminates against someone

2. whether people complain about coworkers not speaking English

3. whether customers of the business speak the other language

6. ***Understanding reference*** *is an important reading skill. What previous words in the sentence do the underlined words refer to?*

How should an employer handle a situation <u>where</u> (_situation_)
(a)

all employees speak English, but two employees insist on speaking to

<u>each other</u> (_____) in another language and their
(b)

coworkers complain about <u>it</u> (_____)? Implementing
(c)

language restrictions in the workplace isn't absolutely illegal. <u>It</u>

(_____) depends on how restrictive the rule is and
(d)

your reasons for implementing <u>it</u> (_____).
(e)

The bank had received numerous complaints from non-

Spanish-speaking coworkers. They complained that a hostile

environment was created when the Hispanic employees talked about

<u>them</u> (_____) and made fun of them in Spanish. The
(f)

four employees sued the bank. They claimed that an English-only

rule discriminated against <u>them</u> (_____) because
(g)

of their national origin and race. The law does not protect an em-

ployee's right to speak <u>his/her</u> (_____) native tongue
(h)

on the job. In another case, however, a store was ordered to change

its English-only policy. <u>They</u> (_____) were allowed to
(i)

require English only when employees were "dealing directly with

a customer."

Examine carefully the reasons why you want to implement such a

rule. Does <u>it</u> (_____) solve or fulfill a legitimate
(j)

business need?

7. *Learning how to rephrase information in your own words from a reading is an important reading skill called* **paraphrasing**. *Complete the following sentences with information from "Frequently Asked Questions." Use your own words.*

a. Everyone speaks English, but the company has two problems:

_____ and _____.

b. In the bank situation, there were two conditions when English

was not required: when _____ or

_____.

c. The bank implemented its policy because non-Spanish-speaking

_____.

d. The court said that the bank's policy was _____ illegal

because _____.

e. In another court decision, a store was only able to _____

when _____.

Targeting

....

Ways to Express Demands

There are different ways to express demands in English. When you use expressions of urgency or importance, pay careful attention to the verb form.

1. *Study these possibilities for expressing demands.*

Structures	**Examples**
insist/demand/require that [someone] **do** [something]	The company **insisted that** he **speak** only English.
NOTE: Be careful not to put a final *-s* on the verb in a noun clause following a demand.	They **demanded that** he **not use** his own language.

Structures	Examples
allow/tell/require/order [someone] **to do** [something]	The supervisor **told** everyone **not to speak** their own languages at work.
	They **allowed** us **to speak** our own languages at lunch.
make [someone] **do** [something]	The company **made** him **speak** English all the time.
It is [important/essential/ necessary/mandatory] **that** [someone] **do** [something].	**It is** essential **that** he **speak** English at work.
It is [important/essential/ necessary/illegal/mandatory] **to do** [something].	**It is** mandatory **to speak** English at work.
Doing [something] **is** [essential/required/ mandatory/necessary/ prohibited].	**Speaking** English at work **is** required.
[someone] **should not be required to do** [something]	No one **should be required to speak** English all the time.
Doing [something] **makes** [someone] **feel/act** . . .	**Requiring** English **makes** some employees **feel** less valued.

2. *Complete these sentences.*

a. The bank ordered its employees _____.

b. Sometimes _____ Spanish was necessary, however.

c. When the customer spoke Spanish, the bank allowed _____

_____.

d. In many companies swearing is _____ , so the

court decided that speaking English could also be prohibited.

e. Another court ordered _____ .

f. The store was allowed _____ only when

employees were dealing directly with customers.

g. When the employees were talking with customers, the store

could require that _____ .

h. Some employees feel that a company should be _____

pay for English lessons if they demand _____

their employees _____ English at work.

i. In my opinion, employees _____ required to

speak English at all times.

j. One court ruled that _____ illegal to _____

_____ all employees to speak English at all times.

Writing

....

Preparing to Write: Planning a Response

How would you respond if you disagreed with a company policy? Your choice of words, tone, and general approach to the situation would be critical. In this section, you will write a response to an English-only policy.

1. *You work at a hospital as a medical technician and speak English as your second language. A friend of yours who works in the hospital cafeteria has asked you to help her write a letter responding to the following policy memo. Read the memo.*

MEMO

TO: All Employees

FROM: Anna Hagelund, Cafeteria Manager

RE: Native Language Use

The cafeteria management has decided to implement an English-only policy. Only English may be spoken unless another language is needed to communicate with a customer.

Failure to comply with this policy will result in a warning. Further failure may result in an employee's being disciplined or losing his or her job.

2. List possible reasons why the manager implemented this policy.

_____

_____

3. List reasons why your friend would think this policy is unfair and/or illegal.

_____

_____

4. Consider the suggestions in the article in chapter 4 on "win-win" negotiating styles on pages 39–40. Is there any way to apply that information to this situation? Make an outline of your letter on separate paper. Be sure to include an introduction to the problem and a possible solution or request.

A formal letter follows business letter format. For examples of **business letter format**, see pages 205–206 in Reference.

Writing a Formal Request

Now write a formal letter requesting that the English-only policy be changed.

Editing and Rewriting

Editing for Errors in Article Use

Whenever you use a noun, you need to decide whether to use *a/an*, *the*, or no article at all.

1. *Here are some rules to remember when you make choices about articles.*

Rules	Examples
Count nouns are nouns that can be singular or plural.	**a** friend, **two** friends, **this** book, my English book**s**
Remember that a **count noun** can never be bare or stand alone.	**INCORRECT** There are problem here. I have problem. Problem is serious. What is problem? We solved problem.
The count noun needs to be "covered" by a plural ending or a determiner.	**CORRECT** *Add a plural ending:* There are problem**s** here.
A determiner gives information about a noun. Typical determiners are articles, possessives, demonstratives, and quantifiers.	*Add a determiner:* I have **a** problem. *(article)* **Our** problem is serious. *(possessive)* What is **this** problem? *(demonstrative)* We solved **every** problem. *(quantifier)*
Adjectives give **extra** information about nouns, but they are not determiners.	**INCORRECT** They are **serious** problem. **CORRECT** They are serious problem**s**.

Rules	Examples
If you have a bare count noun in your writing, something is wrong. Ask yourself: 1. What can I add to "cover" this noun? 2. Is the noun really plural? (Add a plural ending.) 3. If the noun is really singular, can I add a determiner? Which determiner?	**INCORRECT** **CORRECT** We are friend. ⟶ We are friend**s**. I have friend. ⟶ I have **a** friend. He's friend. ⟶ He's **my** friend.
If the determiner is an article, decide whether to use **a** or **the**. When a noun is specific, use **the**. A noun is specific • when it is mentioned the second time or when additional information is given about it. • when you and your listener or reader share an understanding of the noun.	A typical problem is lack of communication. **The** problem only gets worse if you don't try to communicate. *(second mention)* The purpose of **the** new policy was to reduce friction, but it actually made things worse. *(additional information)* I applied for a promotion, but I didn't get **the** job. *(shared understanding)* I'll see you at **the** meeting. *(shared understanding)*
When a noun is not specific or when you are speaking in general • use **a** for a singular count noun. • use **no article** for a noncount noun or for a plural count noun.	This is not **a** problem. *(singular count noun)* **Communication** can be difficult. *(noncount noun)* **Problems** keep coming up. *(plural count noun)*

For more information about noncount nouns and plural nouns, see page 211 in Reference.

For more information about noncount nouns and plural nouns, see page 211 in Reference.

2. *Write **a/an** or **the**, where necessary, in the following paragraphs.*

One of _____ (a) people in my team at

_____ (b) work is unhappy because he didn't get

selected for _____ (c) promotion. He told me that

_____ (d) supervisor didn't give him _____ (e)

job because he has _____ (f) very strong accent. He is

from India and speaks English perfectly. However, his intonation is

different, so it is hard to understand him sometimes.

He talked to _____ (g) lawyer to find out if this

is _____ (h) discrimination. _____ (i)

lawyer said that _____ (j) answer depends on the

situation. If the job requires that _____ (k) people

understand him clearly, then _____ (l) clear language

is mandatory. That is true in this situation because he applied to be

_____ (m) supervisor. However, _____ (n)

company needs to prove that my friend is not understandable. They

will need to provide _____ (o) evidence that he could

not perform _____ (p) job because of his accent.

Editing Checklist

Check the Content

1. *Exchange your letter with a classmate. After you read your classmate's work, answer these questions:*

   ❏ What is the tone of the letter? Do you think the manager will be willing to cooperate with the request?

   ❏ Are the reasons for the request clearly stated?

Check the Details

2. *Read your own letter again. If necessary, make the tone more cooperative and the demands more indirect. Clarify any unclear reasons. Then continue checking your paper. Use these questions:*

   ❏ Are all your sentences complete?

   ❏ Did you use transition and repetition expressions to connect ideas?

   ❏ Check your verb forms for correct subject-verb agreement and tense.

3. *Revise your writing.*

Vocabulary Log

What words or phrases would you like to remember from this chapter? Write five to ten items in your notebook.

Grammar and Punctuation Review

Look over your writing from this chapter. What changes did you need to make in grammar and punctuation? Write them in your notebook. Review them before the next writing assignment.

Chapter 6

The Gender Debate

Why do men and women sometimes have trouble communicating? You will read what one expert thinks and then find out why some people disagree with her. Then you will write a summary of the debate.

Starting Point

Is There a Difference?

1. *Consider this conversation. What differences do you notice between the woman's way of communicating and the man's?*

   WOMAN: Would you like to go out for dinner this weekend?
   MAN: No, I have a golf tournament.
   WOMAN: Well, Sunday night is free. That would work, wouldn't it?
   MAN: Next weekend will be better.

2. *Discuss these questions with your classmates.*

   a. Is there a difference between the way men and women speak in your native language? If so, give examples.

   b. In general, do you think men or women are more likely to be concerned or involved in the following things? Circle *Men* or *Women*.

Maintaining their status in a hierarchy	Men	Women
Establishing a feeling of intimacy	Men	Women
Finding compromises in conflicts	Men	Women
Issuing orders	Men	Women

   c. In work situations, do you think men and women should use the same styles of communicating?

Reading 1

Differences in Communication Styles

There has been a lot of research about the differences between men's and women's communication styles.

1. *Deborah Tannen is a sociolinguistics professor at Georgetown University and the author of several books about the way men and women communicate. Read this excerpt from her book,* You Just Don't Understand: Women and Men in Conversation.

It Begins at the Beginning

Even if they grow up in the same neighborhood, on the same block, or in the same house, girls and boys grow up in different worlds of words. Others talk to them differently and expect and accept different ways of talking from them. Most important, children learn how to talk, how to have conversations, not only from their parents but from their peers. After all, if their parents have a foreign or regional accent, children do not emulate it; they learn to speak with the pronunciation of the region where they grow up. Anthropologists Daviel Maltz and Ruth Borker summarize research showing that boys and girls have very different ways of talking to their friends. Although they often play together, boys and girls spend most of their time playing in same-sex groups. And, although some of the activities they play at are similar, their favorite games are different, and their ways of using language in their games are separated by a world of difference.

Boys tend to play outside, in large groups that are hierarchically structured. Their groups have a leader who tells others what to do and how to do it, and resists doing what other boys propose. It is by giving orders and making them stick that high status is negotiated. Another way boys achieve status is to take center stage by telling stories and jokes, and by side-tracking or challenging the stories and jokes of others. Boys' games have winners and losers and elaborate systems of rules that are frequently the subjects of arguments. Finally, boys are frequently heard to boast of their skill and argue about who is best at what.

Girls, on the other hand, play in small groups or in pairs; the center of a girl's social life is a best friend. Within the group, intimacy is key: differentiation is measured by relative closeness. In their most frequent games, such as jump rope and hopscotch, everyone gets a turn. Many of their activities (such as playing house) do not have winners or losers. Though some girls are certainly more skilled than others, girls are expected not to boast about it, or show that they think they are better than the others. Girls don't give orders; they express their preferences as suggestions, and suggestions are likely to be accepted. Whereas boys say, "Gimme that!" and "Get outta here!" girls say, "Let's do this," and "How about doing that?" Anything else is put down as "bossy." They don't grab center stage—they don't want it—so they don't challenge each other directly. And much of the time, they simply sit together and talk. Girls are not accustomed to jockeying for status in an obvious way; they are more concerned that they be liked.

Gender differences in ways of talking have been described by researchers observing children as young as three. Amy Sheldon videotaped three- to four-year-old boys and girls playing in threesomes at a day-care center. She compared two groups of three—one of boys, one of girls—that got in fights about the same play item: a plastic pickle. Though both groups fought over the same thing, the dynamics by which they negotiated their conflicts were different. In addition to illustrating some of the patterns I have just described, Sheldon's study also demonstrates the complexity of these dynamics.

While playing in the kitchen area of the day-care center, a little girl named Sue wanted the pickle that Mary had, so she argued that Mary should give it up because Lisa, the third girl, wanted it. This led to a conflict about how to satisfy Lisa's (invented) need. Mary proposed a compromise, but Sue protested:

> **MARY:** I cut it in half. One for Lisa, one for me, one for me.
>
> **SUE:** But, Lisa wants a *whole* pickle.

Mary comes up with another creative compromise, which Sue also rejects:

> **MARY:** Well, it's a whole *half* pickle.
>
> **SUE:** No, it isn't.
>
> **MARY:** Yes, it is, a whole *half* pickle.
>
> **SUE:** I'll give her a whole half. I'll give her a *whole whole*. I'll give her a whole one.

At this point, Lisa withdraws from the alliance with Sue, who satisfies herself by saying, "I'm pretending I gave you one."

On another occasion, Sheldon videotaped three boys playing in the same kitchen play area, and they too got into a fight about the plastic pickle. When Nick saw that Kevin had the pickle, he demanded it for himself:

> **NICK:** [Screams] Kevin, but the, oh, I *have* to cut! I want to cut it! It's mine!

Like Sue, Nick involved the third child in his effort to get the pickle:

> **NICK:** [Whining to Joe] Kevin is not letting me cut the pickle.
>
> **JOE:** Oh, I know! I can pull it away from him and give it back to you. That's an idea!

The boys' conflict, which lasted two and a half times longer than the girls', then proceeded as a struggle between Nick and Joe on the one hand and Kevin on the other.

In comparing the boys' and girls' fights, Sheldon points out that, for the most part, the girls mitigated the conflict and preserved harmony by compromise and evasion. Conflict was more prolonged among the boys, who used more insistence, appeals to rules, and threats of physical violence. However, to say that these little girls and boys used *more* of one strategy or another is not to say that they didn't use the other strategies at all. For example, the boys did attempt compromise, and the girls did attempt physical force. The girls, like the boys, were struggling for control of the play. When Sue says by mistake, "*I'll* give her a whole half," then quickly corrects herself to say, "I'll give her a *whole whole*," she reveals that it is not really the size of the portion that is important to her, but who gets to serve it.

While reading Sheldon's study, I noticed that whereas both Nick and Sue tried to get what they wanted by involving a third child, the alignments they created with the third child, and the dynamics they set in motion, were fundamentally different. Sue appealed to Mary to fulfill someone else's desire; rather than saying that *she* wanted the pickle, she claimed that Lisa wanted it. Nick asserted his own desire for the pickle, and when he couldn't get it on his own, he appealed to Joe to get it for him. Joe then tried to get the pickle by force. In both these scenarios, the children were enacting complex lines of affiliation.

Joe's strong-arm tactics were undertaken not on his own behalf but, chivalrously, on behalf of Nick. By making an appeal in a whining voice, Nick positioned himself as one-down in a hierarchical structure, framing himself as someone in need of protection. When Sue appealed to Mary to relinquish her pickle, she wanted to take the one-up position of serving food. She was fighting not for the right to *have* the pickle, but for the right to *serve* it. [...] But to accomplish her goal, Sue was depending on Mary's desire to fulfill others' needs.

This study suggests that boys and girls both want to get their way, but they tend to do so differently. Though social norms encourage boys to be openly competitive and girls to be openly cooperative, different situations and activities can result in different ways of behaving. Marjorie Harness Goodwin compared boys and girls engaged in two task-oriented activities. The boys were making slingshots in preparation for a fight, and the girls were making rings. She found that the boys' group was hierarchical:

the leader told the others what to do and how to do it. The girls' group was egalitarian: everyone made suggestions and tended to accept the suggestions of others. But observing the girls in a different activity—playing house—Goodwin found that they too adopted hierarchical structures: the girls who played mothers issued orders to the girls playing children, who in turn sought permission from their play-mothers. Moreover, a girl who was a play-mother was also a kind of manager of the game. This study shows that girls know how to issue orders and operate in a hierarchical structure, but they don't find that mode of behavior appropriate when they engage in task activities with their peers. They do find it appropriate in parent-child relationships, which they enjoy practicing in the form of play.

These worlds of play shed light on the world views of women and men in relationships. The boys' play illuminates why men would be on the lookout for signs they are being put down or told what to do. The chief commodity that is bartered in the boys' hierarchical world is status, and the way to achieve and maintain status is to give orders and get others to follow them. A boy in a low-status position finds himself being pushed around. So boys monitor their relations for subtle shifts in status by keeping track of who's giving orders and who's taking them.

These dynamics are not the ones that drive girls' play. The chief commodity that is bartered in the girls' community is intimacy. Girls monitor their friendships for subtle shifts in alliance, and they seek to be friends with popular girls. Popularity is a kind of status, but it is founded on connection.

2. *Look at the words on the left. Consider the **context** in which they are used in the reading. Choose the best meaning from the choices in the right-hand column.*

Word from Reading 1	Meaning		
a. [1] peers	grandparents	other children	parent's friends
b. [1] emulate	copy	show	try
c. [2] hierarchically	in a group of equals	with different levels of power and control	with a leader
d. [2] elaborate	clear	complicated	group
e. [2] boast	talk about with pride	criticize someone else's possession	communicate about
f. [3] intimacy	importance of a relationship	difference	feeling of closeness
g. [4] dynamics	the relationships between people	the way people relate	fight
h. [5, third sentence] compromise	solution	solution where each gives up something	promise not to do something again
i. [7] mitigated	made it less serious	solved the problem	continued the situation
j. [9] relinquish	give up	take	forget about

> **READING TIP**
>
> When you read, you use many different strategies to figure out vocabulary. You may try to guess from other information in the reading (the context). You may use your knowledge of related words, affixes, and word roots, or you may use your knowledge of the subject. All of these strategies are part of the skill of **analyzing vocabulary**.

3. *Look back at the selection "It Begins at the Beginning" on pages 61–62. Which of the following express the **main idea** of the paragraphs? Which are **specific details**? Write MI or SD on the line.*

Paragraph 1

a. _____ Tannen believes that boys and girls learn to communicate in different ways from an early age.

b. _____ Although they often play together, boys and girls spend most of their time playing in same-sex groups.

Paragraph 3

c. _____ Being best friends and having no winners or losers are examples of girls' focus on intimacy.

d. _____ Girls are not accustomed to jockeying for status in an obvious way; they are more concerned that they be liked.

Paragraph 6

e. _____ In the same situation, boys argued longer and their dispute involved a physical struggle.

f. _____ The boys' conflict, which lasted two and a half times longer than the girls', then proceeded as a struggle between Nick and Joe on the one hand and Kevin on the other.

Paragraph 11

g. _____ The chief commodity that is bartered in the boys' hierarchical world is status, and the way to achieve and maintain status is to give orders and get others to follow them.

h. _____ A boy in a low-status position finds himself being pushed around.

4. *Summarize* the main points of the reading by *taking notes in this chart*.

Characteristics of the Ways Boys and Girls Communicate

Girls

- _____
- _____
- _____
- _____
- _____
- _____

Boys

- _____
- _____
- _____
- _____
- _____
- _____

Reflect on Reading

Here are some typical ways to organize paragraphs and essays. Which technique(s) best describe(s) the **organization** of "It Begins at the Beginning?"

a. one topic with facts or examples to support it

b. steps in a process or sequence; a list of points in chronological order or in order of importance

c. emphasis on the reasons and/or the results

d. similarities and/or differences

How academic or formal is the style of the selection? Could a student hand in something in this style to a professor? What would need to be different?

Reading 2

The Debate

Now you will read what several other writers have to say about communication between men and women. As you read, try to analyze each writer's point of view. Is it the same as Deborah Tannen's point of view or different?

Characteristics of Women's Language

Numerous traits have been said to characterize women's forms of speech in this culture. Not all women use them, and probably no one uses them all the time. (They are, for instance, more likely to show up in informal social circumstances than in business settings.)

- **Women make more use of expressive forms (adjectives not nouns or verbs and, in that category, those expressing emotional rather than intellectual evaluation) more than men: *lovely, divine*.**
- **Women use forms that convey impreciseness: *so, such*.**
- **Women use intonation patterns that resemble questions, indicating uncertainty or need for approval.**
- **Women are more indirect and polite than men.**
- **Women won't commit themselves to an opinion.**

Robin Lakoff
from *Talking and Power: The Politics of Language*, 1990

---

1. *Circle the letter of the **main idea** for the selection.*

    a. Lakoff's assertions that women use different communication styles from men support Tannen's research.

    b. Lakoff's assertions differ significantly from Tannen's research in that Tannen looked at the differences between communication styles of men and of women.

Job responsibilities can dictate style. [When I led international delegations,] my style of inclusiveness had nothing to do with my being female…[but] with the fact that each of the 80 men on my side of the table had the power to sink the outcome of any negotiation. On the other hand, when I work with enlisted men, I take a militaristic, hierarchical stance.

Rozanne Ridgeway
former U.S. ambassador to Finland in a speech at a roundtable on female leadership styles sponsored by Sara Lee

---

2. *Circle the letter of the **main idea** for the selection.*

    a. Rozanne Ridgeway, a former ambassador, believes that women switch styles of communicating according to their position within a group and the situation.

    b. Rozanne Ridgeway, a former ambassador, emphasizes the need to influence men by using an inclusive style, which had nothing to do with her being female.

> The emphasis on female management style is […] simplistic. All the studies give contradictory results; they were done with young college students, and what they have measured are, in fact, very tiny differences. Most of the studies have not been borne out by research. In fact, all the evidence indicates that there is more variation between people than between sexes.
>
> Cynthia Fuchs Epstein, sociologist and author of *Deceptive Distinctions*.

3. *Circle the letter of the **main idea** for the selection.*

    a. Cynthia Fuchs Epstein, another researcher and author, agrees with Tannen that there is more variation between people than between sexes. She states that research does not support the idea that gender is more important than individual differences in communication.

    b. Cynthia Fuchs Epstein, another researcher and author, disputes Tannen's findings, arguing that research does not support the idea that gender is more important than individual differences in communication.

> I think to focus on difference is to grab the wrong end of the stick. This information about women's behaviors will be translated to the detriment of women. The inevitable effect of the 'feminine' style will be stereotyping. And in the end, all stereotypes are limiting—be they positive or negative. They are disabling, divisive. Women must be empowered to develop personal styles that allow them to be effective.
>
> Sheila Wellington
> Director of *Catalyst*, a corporate-research firm that focuses on women's issues

4. *Circle the letter of the **main idea** for the selection.*

  a. Sheila Wellington, another woman with a strong interest in women's issues, finds fault with Tannen's emphasis on differences and the resulting stereotyping because Wellington believes that stereotyping will hurt women.

  b. Sheila Wellington, another woman with a strong interest in women's issues, agrees with Tannen's emphasis on differences and the resulting stereotyping because Wellington believes that stereotypes are limiting.

5. *What is your opinion of Tannen's research? Discuss this with your classmates.*

6. *Consider these words from the reading. Cross out the word that does not belong in each group.*

a. negative	harm	disabling	empowered
b. characteristics	criticism	traits	qualities
c. informal	social	business	easygoing
d. indirect	imprecise	clear	flowery
e. militaristic	egalitarian	hierarchical	with different levels of power
f. difference	stereotype	individualistic	variation
g. researcher	author	ambassador	expert
h. assert	claim	question	state
i. isolation	communication	interaction	conversation
j. establish	build	create	mainstream

Targeting Collocations

Verbs to Report Point of View

In many different types of academic writing (reports, summary, comments about data), you will need to report what studies show or what people believe.

1. *Study the verbs and expressions.*

Verbs and Expressions	Examples
Many point-of-view verbs are followed by a noun clause beginning with *that*. affirm conclude agree/disagree contend argue emphasize assert explain believe maintain claim say state	She *believes* **that women use** different communication styles from men. They *agree* **that boys and girls have** different styles of communicating, but they *contend* **that these differences result** from different ways that parents and society treat boys and girls.
Other point-of-view verbs are followed by a noun, which is sometimes followed by an adjective clause beginning with *that*. accept emphasize affirm examine attack explain cite find criticize question	Their article *criticized* **the research**.
agree/disagree with [someone/someone's idea] **about** [something]	Many feminists *disagree with* Tannen **about** the degree to which men's and women's communication styles differ.
find fault with [the idea] **that**	He *found fault with the idea* **that women's language is** different than men's.
criticize [someone] **for** [noun/doing something]	Crawford *criticizes* Tannen **for** implying that women are weaker than men.
question/debate/doubt/dispute [noun]/**whether** [one thing is true]	Crawford *doubts* **whether** the research is valid. They **are debating the issue** in articles in academic journals.

ANSWER KEY

2. *Match the partial sentences. There may be more than one answer possible.*

a. Crawford says _____

b. Crawford criticizes Tannen _____

c. Crawford attacks _____

d. She argues _____

e. She debates _____

f. She questions _____

1. the validity of the research.

2. whether the explanation for how we behave is in our nature or in our environment.

3. for her failure to analyze the power issues involved in speech and the impact of role and status.

4. Tannen's implication that there is something essentially female in submissive, blurred language.

5. that Tannen has failed to analyze the power issues involved in speech and the impact of role and status.

6. that the researchers are ignoring factors of age, social class, and sexual orientation.

3. *Use each of the verbs below in a sentence of your own. Express your own or someone else's point of view about the way that men and women communicate.*

disagree   doubt   criticize   find   question

Writing

Preparing to Write: Steps for Writing a Summary

The steps in this section will help you write a summary, your next writing task.

1. *You are going to write a summary of the debate that you have read about in this chapter. First, look over the readings and the main ideas you found in doing the exercises. Which of the following would be a good way to introduce the debate summary? Circle the letter.*

a. There is a great deal of debate about differences in communicating styles between men and women.

b. Do the differences in men's and women's communication styles come from childhood and their basic natures or do they come from the roles men and women have as adults?

c. Many psychologists and linguists have written about the differences between men's and women's styles of communication.

2. *As you summarize each point of view, you will need to write an introduction to that idea. Each of these sentences will contain three parts:*

a. the name of the person and the source of the information

b. a reporting verb (see page 69)

c. the main idea (that person's point of view)

Here are examples of some common ways to introduce the source:

In her book, <u>You Just Don't Understand</u>, Deborah Tannen claims that . . .

Deborah Tannen, in her book, <u>You Just Don't Understand</u>, claims that . . .

According to an Emory University study, . . .

This study suggests that . . .

The article, "Language and Woman's Place," by Robin Lakoff examines whether . . .

Write an introduction that states the source of the first point of view in your summary.

_____

_____

3. *Now continue to summarize Tannen's point of view. You may want to use some of the main idea statements in exercises 2–4 on pages 63–65 or your notes on page 65.*

_____

_____

_____

READING TIP

Add transition and repetition words to connect your ideas. See pages 212–214 for examples.

4. *How might you introduce the ideas in "Characteristics of Women's Language"? Write an introduction to this part of your summary.*

_____

5. *Summarize the points of view in "Characteristics of Women's Language." The main idea exercises on pages 66–68 may help you.*

6. *Write a conclusion to your summary. This may be your opinion or just a final sentence about what you have written.*

Writing a Summary

Now you are ready to write a summary of the debate on communication styles and gender. Use your answers from Preparing to Write: Steps for Writing a Summary to help you.

_____

_____

_____

_____

_____

_____

_____

_____

_____

Editing and Rewriting

Editing for Sentence Completeness

Sometimes it is difficult to decide if a sentence is complete or not.

1. *Study these facts about sentences.*

Rules	Examples	
A complete sentence has a subject and a verb.	**INCORRECT** Their communication styles.	**CORRECT** Their communication styles **differ**.
Words like "that," "who," and "because" can connect two ideas that have their own subject and verb.	**INCORRECT** The idea **that** girls and boys learn different styles as children. *(The main idea is missing.)*	**CORRECT** **She disagreed with the idea that** girls and boys learn different styles as children.

Rules	Examples	
	INCORRECT	**CORRECT**
Two complete sentences cannot be connected by a comma only. Separate them into two sentences or connect them with a conjunction, a transition word, or a semicolon.	Girls play in small groups or in pairs, the center of a girl's social life is a best friend.	Girls play in small groups or in pairs, **and** the center of a girl's social life is a best friend.
		Girls play in small groups or in pairs; **in fact**, the center of a girl's social life is a best friend.
		Girls play in small groups or in pairs; the center of a girl's social life is a best friend.

2. *Correct the errors in sentence completeness, where necessary.*

a. The way that men and women communicate very different.

b. Sometimes women use styles that are more typically male. For example when they speak forcefully and directly.

c. When women use more masculine communication styles, people are shocked.

d. People are shocked. Because they don't expect women to be so forceful.

e. That women and men communicate differently.

f. The fact is that people are all different.

g. Some people disagree with Tannen's ideas, they think that women change their style depending on the situation.

h. I think that women should not change their communication style, they are able to be successful in any situations with their own styles.

i. Tannen believes that men and women different.

j. Research shows girls can switch styles. Because they use hierarchical styles when they play the roles of family members.

Editing Checklist

Check the Content

1. *Exchange your summary with a classmate. After you read your classmate's work, answer these questions:*

   ❏ Is there an introduction and a conclusion?
   ❏ Are the different points of view clearly stated?

Check the Details

2. *Read your own summary again. If necessary, add an introduction or conclusion or clarify a point of view. Then continue checking your paper. Use these questions:*

   ❏ Are all your sentences complete?
   ❏ Did you use transition and repetition expressions to connect ideas?
   ❏ Check your verb forms for correct subject-verb agreement and tense.

3. *Revise your writing.*

Vocabulary Log

What words or phrases would you like to remember from this chapter? Write five to ten items in your notebook.

Grammar and Punctuation Review

Look over your writing from this chapter. What changes did you need to make in grammar and punctuation? Write them in your notebook. Review them before the next writing assignment.

Class Activity

Work in a group. Choose one of these topics for discussion.

1 Are there levels of politeness in your language? Teach the class some important phrases to know when speaking to people in your country; for example, to someone older, to a child, or to a man versus a woman.

2 Are there differences between men's and women's communication styles in your language? Brainstorm some words or grammar structures that one gender is more likely to say. Do a survey of other speakers from your language and report to the class.

3 Research language policies in the business world. You may find information about this on the Internet or in the library. Share your results with the class.

3 Personality Plus

What makes one person happy while another is sad? Is there any way to predict how well people will get along with each other? These are some of the activities you will do in this unit:

- Read about whether scientists believe there is a gene that determines happiness

- Write essay exam responses

- Read about predicting successful relationships

- Write a paper about emotions and personality

Chapter 7

A Happiness Gene?

Some researchers believe that happiness, at least in part, is determined by genes. In this chapter you will read a textbook selection about this issue and answer essay exam questions that might appear on a test.

....

Starting Point

A Happiness Quiz

How happy do you think you are? Take this quiz to find out!

Circle the letter of the answer that matches your situation most closely.

A Happiness Quiz

How happy do you think you are? Take this quiz and find out!

Circle the letter of the answer that matches your situation most closely.

1. How busy is your life?
   a. I can never catch up with everything I have to do.
   b. I'm busy, but I have time to relax.
   c. I have too much free time.

2. How much is new in your life?
   a. I have had a major change in my life recently.
   b. There haven't been any major changes in my life recently.

3. How healthy are you?
   a. I have had to stay home because of illness more than twice in the past six months.
   b. I haven't had to stay home because of illness very much recently.

4. How much time do you spend with friends?
   a. I don't see too much of my friends.
   b. I see my friends quite often.
   c. I don't have many friends.

5. How comfortable are you spending time alone?
   a. I don't want to be alone.
   b. I like to be alone occasionally.
   c. I like being alone more than being with other people.

6. How fulfilling are your activities?
   a. I'm busy, but I don't feel like I'm accomplishing very much.
   b. I get a feeling of accomplishment from my activities.

7. How much control do you have over your activities?
   a. I am limited in my choices about how to spend my time.
   b. I can decide how to spend my time.

8. Do you have trouble sleeping?
   a. I have trouble sleeping.
   b. I almost never have trouble sleeping.

Give yourself a point for every b *answer. If your score is less than 4, you are probably anxious and possibly depressed about your life. A score of 4 or more indicates that you may be very happy at this point in your life.*

Reading

Is There a Happiness Gene?

Genes are part of DNA, a person's biological foundation. They determine hereditary characteristics for example, the color of your eyes. This reading selection reports on preliminary research on a link between genes and feelings of happiness.

1. **Preview** *the academic reading by looking at the headings. Which of the following is probably included in the selection? Put a check (✓) on the line.*

   _____ historical information

   _____ characteristics of happy people

   _____ research about the relationship between genes and happiness

   _____ psychological problems of unhappy people

   _____ a research study about criminals

   _____ reasons why some people don't believe the research findings

2. *Now read the selection. As you read, imagine that you are going to have to take a test on this information. Underline or highlight any information you will need to remember for the test.*

READING TIP

Don't worry about words that are unfamiliar. Just keep reading for the general meaning.

GENES AND EMOTIONS

The increase in gene research has led to a debate about the nature of happiness. Some scientists believe that happiness is genetic.

The Twin Study

Behavioral geneticist Dean Hamer believes that there are genes that make some people happier or sadder than others. Hamer reviewed studies of the sense of well-being experienced by sets of twins. In the first study, psychologist David Lykken and Auke Tellegen tried to measure happiness in 1,500 sets of twins, half of whom were identical and the other half fraternal. The researchers used a questionnaire with true-false statements such as "I am just naturally cheerful" and "My future looks bright to me." The responses, or happiness scores, of the fraternal twins were almost no different from the reponses of unrelated pairs of people. The identical twins, however, rated their happiness–or despair–almost the same. Since identical twins share the same genes, the similarity of their results compared to the lack of similarity in the fraternal twins' scores showed a genetic link to happiness.

These researchers also studied a smaller group of identical twins who had been separated at birth and raised in different families. They found that even these identical twins had almost the same feelings of happiness or despair. For example, a man raised in an uneducated fishing family scored the same on the researcher's questionnaire as his twin, whose father by adoption was the head of the police force. The same results were found with twin girls, one of whom grew up in an extremely poor inner city neighborhood while the other grew up in a wealthy area out in the country. This study confirmed the link between genetic similarity and feelings of happiness.

Debate Over the Influence of Genes

Hamer viewed the research on twins as strong proof that people inherit their temperament. People's basic personality is biological, passed down as a pattern of interacting genes. He believes that further research will identify the genes that contribute to the underlying factors leading to happiness. The study on twins did not identify any particular genes, but Hamer suggests that as many as a dozen genes may be involved. The genes may be those known to control the brain chemicals serotonin and dopamine, both associated with pleasure and mood. Scientists believe that depression and anxiety are caused by an imbalance of these.

The two researchers on the twin study, however, do not view their results from such a strict genetic viewpoint. They do not believe that happiness and despair are "preprogrammed" in every human cell. Tellegen believes that the underlying ability to experience pleasure may be genetic, but much of happiness comes from other things such as family, friends, and accomplishment. Lykken also does not believe their research means that genes absolutely determine someone's quality of life. He shares Tellegen's belief that people can influence their feeling of well-being. Counseling such as psychotherapy can help people to change their outlook, and everyday activities such as reading books or gardening can keep people above their happiness "norm."

Hamer's critics say that genes may only indirectly influence some of the similarities in the twin's answers on the questionnaire. Children who are inherently cheerful will have different experiences from children who are inherently anxious or sad. Did these children's genes bring them happiness or did the genes just prompt the type of behavior or experiences that bring happiness?

Harvard psychology professor Jerome Kagan is a leading critic of the twins research. He does not believe that researchers can measure happiness simply by asking people whether they are happy on a questionnaire. People may have some days when they are happier than others. They may also have a tendency to hide their true feelings. Kagan believes that some people inherit a neurochemical tendency to be unhappy. However, to find these people scientifically, the researchers need to observe them rather than just ask them if they are happy.

Traits of Happy People

The researchers' belief that genetic predisposition is only part of the equation is backed up by other research. Studies have shown that even a simple action such as smiling activates some of the pleasure chemicals in the brain. In numerous studies, happy people share four traits. First, happy people like themselves. On questionnaires designed to measure self-esteem, they agree with statements such as "I'm a lot of fun to be with" and "I have good ideas." They also see themselves as more ethical, more intelligent, healthier, and more likeable than other people.

Secondly, happy people feel that they have control over their lives. They feel empowered instead of helpless, so they do better in school and work, and deal with stress better. Research in prisons, nursing homes, and totalitarian countries has shown the depressing effects of the lack of personal control. When people don't have control over their lives, they suffer from depression and poor health. This is also the case when extreme poverty takes away people's feelings of control in their lives.

The third trait that happy people share is optimism. People who agreed with the statement, "When I undertake something new, I expect to succeed," were generally more successful, healthier, and happier.

Fourth, researchers have found that happy people are extroverts. Although researchers expected that introverts would be happier because they had less stress in their more thought-filled and quieter lives, they found that extroverts were happier no matter where they lived or worked.

In summary, the debate continues about whether the ability to be happy is inherited and about the degree to which activities influence happiness.

ANSWER KEY

3. *Circle the best meaning of the underlined word from the **context** of the sentences.*

   a. Counseling such as psychotherapy can help people change their <u>outlook</u>.

   view of the future   vision   personality

   b. Hamer viewed the research on twins as strong <u>proof</u> that people <u>inherit</u> their temperament.

   showing   criticism   evidence

   develop   are born with   hide

   c. The genes may be those known to control the brain chemicals <u>serotonin and dopamine</u>, both associated with pleasure and mood.

   brain chemicals   genes   parts of the brain

   d. First, happy people like themselves. On questionnaires designed to measure <u>self-esteem</u>, they agree with statements such as "I'm a lot of fun to be with" and "I have good ideas."

   positive feelings about oneself   quality of life   happiness

   e. Secondly, happy people feel that they have control over their lives. They feel <u>empowered</u> instead of helpless.

   helpless   in control   energized

   f. Studies have shown that even a simple action such as smiling <u>activates</u> some of the pleasure chemicals in the brain.

   turns on   stops   starts to work

   g. He believes that further research will identify the genes that contribute to the <u>underlying factors</u> leading to happiness.

   background   true reasons   foundation

ANSWER KEY

4. *Decide whether these pairs of words are similar or different. Write S or D on the lines.*

   a. _____ sense of well-being – happiness

   b. _____ identical twins – fraternal twins

   c. _____ cheerful – anxious

   d. _____ happiness – despair

   e. _____ depression – anxiety

   f. _____ birth – adoption

   g. _____ confirm – question

h. _____ view – consider

i. _____ inherently – basically

j. _____ temperament – basic personality

k. _____ underlying – basic

l. _____ extroverts – introverts

5. *What do the underlined words **refer** to?*

In the first study, psychologists David Lykken and Auke Tellegen

tried to measure happiness in 1,500 sets of twins, half of <u>whom</u>

_____ were identical and <u>the other half</u>
(a)

_____ fraternal. For example, a man raised in an
(b)

uneducated fishing family scored the same on the researchers'

questionnaire as <u>his</u> _____ twin, <u>whose</u>
(c)

_____ father by adoption was the head of a police
(d)

force. The same results were found with twin girls, one of <u>whom</u>

_____ grew up in an extremely poor inner city
(e)

neighborhood while <u>the other</u> _____ grew up
(f)

in a wealthy area out in the country. The genes may be <u>those</u>

_____ known to control the brain chemicals
(g)

serotonin and dopamine, <u>both</u> _____ associated
(h)

with pleasure and mood. Scientists believe that depression and

anxiety are caused by an imbalance of <u>these</u> _____ .
(i)

<u>The researchers'</u> _____ belief that genetic predis-
(j)

position is only part of the equation is backed up by other research.

ANSWER KEY

6. An **inference** is something you understand from a reading, but the writer doesn't state directly. Put a check next to the items that you can **infer** from the reading.

   a. _____ Hamer probably does other research studying genes.

   b. _____ Lykken and Tellegen's study showed that fraternal twins shared the same degree of happiness.

   c. _____ The impact of heredity on happiness was stronger than the impact of environment in the study of identical twins.

   d. _____ Hamer knows which genes are involved.

   e. _____ Lykken and Tellegen believe that genes will always determine how happy a person will be.

   f. _____ People criticize Hamer, but not Lykken and Tellegen.

   g. _____ Kagan thinks that there is a biological factor that affects levels of happiness.

   h. _____ Kagan criticized the study as being unscientific.

   i. _____ Someone in a country with a strong dictator is more likely to be depressed than someone in a democracy.

7. When you study for a test, it helps to predict the most likely questions. What questions do you think a professor would be likely to ask about "Genes and Emotions"? Write them on separate paper. Then give them to your classmates. See if they can answer them.

Quickwriting

Happy or Not?

Are you generally a happy person? Are you an optimist or a pessimist? What do you think contributes to your outlook? In your notebook, write for five to ten minutes on this topic.

Targeting

Prefixes and Roots

ANSWER KEY

Learning common prefixes and roots in English helps you decode the meanings of unfamiliar words more quickly.

1. Look at the definitions of the words on the next page with the same prefix. What do you think each of the prefixes means?

Definitions	Prefixes
community: a group of people sharing a common location or interests **converge:** to tend to go toward a common point **collective:** of or pertaining to people working as a group	**a.** *col/com-* means _____
psychological: of or involving the mind or emotions **psychiatry:** the medical study, diagnosis, treatment, and prevention of mental illness **psychic:** pertaining to the human mind or psyche	**b.** *psych-* means _____
similarity: likeness **simulate:** to take on the appearance of; imitate	**c.** *simi-* means _____
profoundly: completely; deeply **foundation:** the basis or ground-work of anything **fundamental:** elemental; basic	**d.** *found/fund-* means _____
empathy: understanding the feelings of another **sympathy:** feeling sorrow for another	**e.** *path-* means _____
technique: procedure using skills **technology:** the application of scientific skills **technician:** someone skilled in a technique or technology	**f.** *techno-* means _____

Definitions	Prefixes
multicultural: having many cultures **multitude:** a great, indefinite number **multiply:** to increase in number	**g.** *multi-* means _____ OR _____
universal: worldwide; affecting everyone **universally:** affecting everyone in the same way **unity:** the state of being one	**h.** *uni-* means _____ OR _____
malice: ill will with a desire to harm **malevolent:** having ill will; having a bad influence **malign:** to speak evil of **malignant:** highly injurious; damaging	**i.** *mal-* means _____ OR _____
oppose: to place against **position:** place or location **posit:** to put forward as truth	**j.** *pos-* means _____ OR _____

Writing

Preparing to Write 1: Understanding Essay Exam Questions

When you take essay exams, you need to write carefully organized answers that show you understand the course material. You also have a limited amount of time to write. Your first step in preparing to write is to analyze the question.

1. *If you found the phrases on the next page in essay exam questions, what kind of paragraph would you write? Label the phrases with these organizational patterns:*

D: definition   CC: comparison/contrast   C-R: cause-result/effect

CL: classification   P: process   EX: examples to prove a generalization

a. <u>C-R</u> What is the effect of . . .

b. _____ What is meant by . . .

c. _____ What are the major differences between . . .

d. _____ Illustrate . . .

e. _____ Discuss the reasons for . . .

f. _____ What are the distinguishing characteristics of . . .

g. _____ What factors contributed to . . .

h. _____ Trace the development of . . .

i. _____ Discuss the advantages of . . . over . . .

j. _____ Give examples to show that . . .

k. _____ How does . . . work

l. _____ How is . . . divided . . .

Preparing to Write 2: Organizing Essay Exam Responses

The second step in essay tests is to organize your response.

- Quickly write down brief notes about the information you will use in your response.
- As you look at your notes, decide what your main point is.
- Begin your answer with a topic sentence that shows that you understand the question. Include a rephrasing of the question in your first sentence.

After you have your topic sentence, your task is to support your main point. Be sure to add enough support. The order and organization of the details you add should be clear from this topic sentence.

1. *Rephrase each question as the topic sentence of your response.*

ANSWER KEY

a. What research procedures did Lykken and Tellegen follow?

Lykken and Tellegen used questionnaires to do
_____

their research.
_____

b. What are the traits of happy people?

_____

_____

c. What does Hamer mean when he says that people inherit a biologically based temperament?

_____

_____

d. What research supports the relationship between genes and emotions?

_____

_____

e. What do critics of the research on the genetic link to happiness believe?

_____

_____

f. Do a person's genes predetermine how happy that person will be?

_____

_____

Writing Essay Exam Responses

Write short answers to the questions in Preparing to Write 2. Use transition words or expressions to connect your ideas. When you take an essay exam, the length of your response will depend on how long your instructor gives you to write. For example, if you have five questions to answer in fifty minutes, your instructor probably expects one paragraph per answer. If you have an hour to answer only one question, you should write at least a five-paragraph essay.

Editing and Rewriting

....

Editing for Punctuation

When you combine ideas, the punctuation is sometimes tricky.

1. *Study these rules.*

Rules	Examples
When two clauses are connected with a subordinating **conjunction**, a comma is not necessary.	People often feel depressed **when** they lack control over their lives.

Rules	Examples
If the subordinating **conjunction** and dependent clause are at the beginning, you need a comma after the clause.	**When** they lack control over their lives, people often feel depressed. **Because** they were extremely poor, they didn't have many options open to them.
Adverbial expressions that begin a sentence or interrupt a sentence are separated with a comma.	**In contrast,** the identical twins' scores were almost identical. **At that point,** they were able to make the connection between genes and feelings of happiness. Their critics, **however,** argue that the research method was unscientific.
A **colon** comes at the end of an independent clause. It introduces a list or information that further explains the first clause.	Happy people share four traits: high self-esteem, control over their lives, optimism, and extroversion. Happy people feel that they have control over their lives: They feel empowered rather than helpless.
Don't use a colon immediately after a verb, preposition, or expression like *such as* or *for example*.	**INCORRECT** The researchers were: David Lykken and Auke Tellegen. Other researchers asked about: self-esteem, happiness, and amount of control. They asked about emotions such as: anger, happiness, and sadness.

Rules	Examples
Semicolons are often used to connect two independent clauses. However, the ideas in the two clauses need to be closely related. Often, the second clause explains the first clause in different words.	Extroverts enjoy socializing; introverts prefer to spend time alone. The questionnaire was very simple; they asked true-false questions.
Semicolons are used with **transitional expressions** that show cause-result, addition, or contrast. Remember that transitional expressions are separated from the rest of the sentence by a comma.	The twins were adopted by two different families; **therefore**, they didn't grow up in the same environment. *(cause-result)* They studied identical twins raised in the same environment; **in addition**, they studied identical twins who had been separated at birth. *(addition)* Their interpretation of the results seems to make sense; **however**, some scientists don't agree with their interpretation. *(contrast)*
Semicolons also separate items in a list when there is a comma in one of the items.	Happy people share four traits: high self-esteem; empowerment, or control over their lives; optimism; and extroversion.

For more information about transition expressions, see Reference, pages 212–214.

2. *Put a check (✓) in front of the sentence(s) with correct punctuation.*

ANSWER KEY

a. _____ In the 1990s, researchers were able to make great progress in gene research.

b. _____ Researchers found a link between depression and lack of empowerment in four situations: prisons, nursing homes, totalitarian countries, and extreme poverty.

c. _____ When they did their research they used a simple questionnaire.

d. _____ Although gene research is recent, people have been trying to figure out the nature of happiness for centuries.

e. _____ The researchers studied a lot of people: including identical twins, fraternal twins, and people who were not related to each other.

f. _____ Identical twins shared the same feelings of well-being: even twins brought up in different families shared the same level of happiness.

g. _____ They studied fraternal and identical twins, in addition they studied identical twins who had been raised in different environments.

h. _____ The research seemed conclusive, however, some other experts question the results.

i. _____ The questionnaire was unscientific; in fact, people could answer however they wanted and hide their true feelings.

j. _____ One thing is definite; more research will be done.

k. _____ They studied four groups: fraternal twins; people who were not related, identical twins, and identical twins brought up in different homes, as the result of adoption.

l. _____ For example they asked how happy people felt in general.

m. _____ Gene research was once unheard of. Now, however, it is one of the most exciting areas of scientific investigation.

n. _____ They did research in: prisons, nursing homes, and totalitarian countries.

Editing Checklist

Check the Content   1. *Exchange your essay exam responses with a classmate. After you read your classmate's work, answer these questions:*

❑ Is there a topic sentence that rephrases the question?
❑ Is there enough support for the topic sentence?
❑ Do transition words or expressions tie the paragraph together?

Check the Details   2. *Read your own writing again. If necessary, revise. Add or change details. Then continue checking your paper. Use these questions:*

❑ Are all your sentences complete?
❑ Did you use transitions and repetition expressions to connect ideas?
❑ Check your verb forms for correct subject-verb agreement and tense.
❑ Is the punctuation correct?

3. *Revise your writing.*

Vocabulary Log

What words or phrases would you like to remember from this chapter? Write five to ten items in your notebook.

Grammar and Punctuation Review

Look over your writing from this chapter. What changes did you need to make in grammar and punctuation? Write them in your notebook. Review them before the next writing assignment.

Class Activity

Work in a group. Choose one of these activities. When you are finished, present your findings to the class.

1 At certain predictable times in life, people may get depressed. Do research on this topic. Investigate stressful times in life and treatment options for people who are depressed.

2 Design your own happiness questionnaire. Conduct a survey and report the results to the class.

Chapter 8

Getting Along

What makes people get along with each other or not? In this chapter you will read and write about this topic.

Starting Point

· ·

Finding Harmony

What makes people get along and work well together? Are certain combinations of people more likely to be successful than others?

1. *Consider the following situations. Match the situation with the heading.*

   Opposites attract.   Blood will tell.

   It's written in the stars.   Great minds think alike.

   Every product-oriented person needs a process-oriented colleague.

   a. _____

   Two young people are on the same sports team. Their horoscopes say that they will get along well together. They want the coach to plan games around the dates that the horoscope says are favorable.

   b. _____

   Two people are getting married. She is extremely outgoing and talkative. He is very quiet and is happiest being by himself.

   c. _____

   Two people are working together on a project. One is concerned with the way that things are being done; the other is more concerned with finishing it, no matter how.

d. _____

A group of coworkers listens carefully to the team leader. Although there is some discussion, everyone is convinced by the leader's ideas.

e. _____

A company reviews employees' physician's reports before assigning people to a team.

2. _Consider the situations in exercise 1 again. Do they have a good chance of success? A doubtful chance of success? Can you make a judgment? Why, or why not?_

· ·

Reading

Predicting Successful Relationships

What kind of personality makes the best coworker? The best friend? The best partner for life?

1. _Read the following selection._

Predicting Successful Relationships

[1] As long as people have interacted, social scientists have tried to categorize different personality types. Hippocrates, in the fifth century B.C., described people according to the four "humours": blood, which caused cheerfulness; black bile, which caused sadness; phlegm, which caused a lack of energy; and yellow bile, which caused anxiety and irritability.

[2] Nowadays, people are more likely to look for less graphic biological traits in people. However, the search to find ways to predict successful relationships is as strong as ever in both work and personal relationships. Magazines offer tests for couples to figure out compatibility based on personality types. Are you a perfectionist, a go-getter, a romantic, an observer, a questioner, a fun lover, a giver, a leader, or a peacemaker? How about your partner? Astrologers offer advice about the best matches based on the position of the stars at birth. However, like Hippocrates,

> **READING TIP**
>
> When you read an article that gives an opinion, think about whether you agree or disagree with the writer. As you read, **analyze the support** that the writer gives.

many people are still searching for a biochemical basis to figure out how people will get along.

[3] Toshitaka Nomi, a Japanese author, has written 30 best-selling books about blood types. According to Nomi, people with type O blood are strong leaders who inspire others with their enthusiasm and optimism. They are very goal oriented, a trait that can also be interpreted as status seeking and greedy. Type A's may be perfectionists. Their characteristics of orderliness and attention to detail can also be seen as negatives (pickiness and inflexibility). Type B's, according to Nomi, are independent, flexible, passionate, and creative. On the other hand, they may also be unpredictable and impatient. Type AB's are considered very organized and honest, but also unforgiving, nitpicky, and conservative. Nomi offers suggestions about which careers are best for which blood types. For example, Nomi thinks that Type A's would make good accountants or librarians while Type B's would make good cooks or journalists.

[4] Some companies and military organizations have formed groups on the basis of similar personalities. However, research indicates that multidimensional work groups may be more effective. A team with similar personalities or cultural backgrounds may work more quickly because the team members will disagree less often, but similar team members may consider fewer ideas. This means that the end result may be less creative. Occasionally, a group convinces itself that it is right even when all signs indicate the opposite. This is called "group think."

[5] Counselors give workshops on how to communicate effectively. For many years, psychologists have said that being a good listener is the most important factor in getting along with people. However, recent research on successful marriages have found that this may not be true. In this study, in the most successful relationships, one person—the husband—gave in to the other's demands. Does this hold true for other relationships (friendships, work teams, partnerships) as well?

[6] The search for the perfect predictor for successful relationships goes on.

2. ***Taking notes*** *as you read is a helpful academic reading skill. Take notes from "Predicting Successful Relationships" using the outline on the next page.*

I. Ways to categorize personality types

A. Historical

    1. Hippocrates

       a. _____

       b. _____

       c. _____

       d. _____

B. Now

    1. magazines

      examples: _____

    2. _____

    3. biochemical basis – Nomi (Japan)

Type O	Positive	Negative
	_____	_____
	_____	_____
Type A	Positive	Negative
	_____	_____
	_____	_____
Type B	Positive	Negative
	_____	_____
	_____	_____
Type AB	Positive	Negative
	_____	_____
	_____	_____

C. Making work groups based on similarities

    Positive _____

    Negative _____

    _____ (group think)

D. Counseling – how to _____

    most important – _____

    new research – _____

READING TIP

When you **take notes**, remember to write a shortened version of the information. For example, use key words and noun phrases rather than complete sentences.

ANSWER KEY

3. **Analyze** *the support that the writer offers in this reading selection. Are the following items references to research or opinions? Write R or O.*

a. Hippocrates _____

b. astrologers _____

c. Nomi _____

d. ideas about multidimensional work teams _____

e. psychologists _____

f. recent ideas about successful marriages _____

ANSWER KEY

4. *Do you know other* **word forms** *related to these from the reading? Complete the chart.*

From the reading	Noun, verb, adjective, or adverb	Another example
scientist	*noun*	*scientific (adj.)*
categorize		
energy		
irritability		
biological		
perfectionist		
compatibility		
inspire		
optimism		
astrologer		

5. Look at the words listed in exercise 4 on page 96. What are typical endings for adjectives, nouns, verbs, and adverbs?

Adjective ending(s):

_____

Noun ending(s) for a person:

_____

Verb ending(s):

_____

Noun ending(s) not for a person:

_____

Adverb ending(s):

_____

6. Knowing **roots and affixes** is important for both reading and writing. Match the partial word meanings and whole-word meanings in chart A to the words in chart B on the next page. Then think of another word using the same part. You may use a partial-word meaning more than once. The first word has been done for you.

A

Partial-word meanings	Whole-word meanings
accomplish, perform	ability to get along
before	able to change easily
bend	communicate with someone
between	condition of being happy
living	condition of being nervous
many	dealing with life processes or living things
mind	having different characteristics
not	know beforehand
person	not agree
quality or condition of	not patient
say	person who deals with personal issues
together	person who studies science
	something that tells what will happen
	unwilling to make any changes
	working well, working as intended

		Partial-word meaning (in bold)	Whole-word meaning	Another example
a.	anxi**ety**	quality or condition of	condition of being nervous	variety
b.	**bio**logical			
c.	cheerful**ness**			
d.	**com**patibility			
e.	**dis**agree			
f.	**effect**ive			
g.	**flex**ible			
h.	**im**patient			
i.	**in**flexible			
j.	**inter**act			
k.	**multi**-dimensional			
l.	**pre**dict			
m.	predi**ctor**			
n.	**psych**ologist			
o.	scient**ist**			

7. *What do you think? Discuss these questions in a small group.*

    a. Which of these might help predict how well people will get along?

        1. astrology

        2. personality tests

        3. blood type

        4. _____
        (Your idea)

    b. Imagine that you had to appoint a group of people to work on a space station. Would you choose people from the same country or from different countries?

    c. If people in this group had trouble getting along, which of these would you do?

        1. hire a counselor to advise them

        2. appoint one person to be the leader and make all the decisions

        3. _____
        (Your idea)

Writing

Preparing to Write 1: Quickwriting

In your next writing assignment, you will write an analysis paper about personality and include supporting details. Quickwriting can help you brainstorm ideas about a specific topic.

1. *Choose one of the following topics.*

    What has been the happiest time of your life? Why?

    Describe the most difficult person you have had to deal with in your life.

    Do you believe blood type or zodiac sign affects personality?

    What has the most significant impact on the development of personality?

2. *Quickwrite for ten minutes on the topic you chose. Remember when you quickwrite to write your thoughts as quickly as you can. Don't worry about details like spelling, grammar, or punctuation. If you don't know a word in English, go ahead and write it in your native language. Don't stop to use the dictionary when you quickwrite.*

Preparing to Write 2: Adding Support

Your writing will be stronger and more interesting if you **provide support** for your ideas. You can use a variety of supporting techniques in your writing.

1. *Study these common kinds of support.*

Kinds of Support	Examples
1. stories, examples, specific details	There was no way to predict how my friend's mother would behave. Sometimes she would be extremely friendly; at other times, she would punish my friend for no apparent reason.
2. facts, statistics, information from an authority	The quality of attention that newborns receive has the greatest impact on the development of their brains and personalities. Researchers studied children who were abandoned in understaffed institutions before being adopted. Brain scans on these children have shown that key regions did not develop in the brains of children who were deprived of early stimulation.
3. reasons, causes and effects	Although every child has a unique personality at birth, parents contribute a great deal to helping a child's personality develop. If children don't get appropriate attention as infants, they will not develop to their full potential.

2. *Read each example. On the line, write the number of the kind of support from the chart above. Some examples may use more than one kind of support.*

a. _____ According to recent research studies using visual records of the developing brain, the most important time in the development of a child's personality is from birth to 18 months.

b. _____ Dan, who was neglected as a baby, hates to be hugged. When someone touches him even gently on the arm, he cringes and gets upset.

c. _____ The period from birth to 18 months is the time when children learn about emotional and social attachments. A child who is left alone to cry will have trouble in later life trusting people.

d. _____ Parts of the brain will shut down if they are not given enough stimulation at early stages of development. A baby with something preventing vision, for example, will remain blind if his or her vision is not repaired before age three. Without early stimulation of the part of the brain that is responsible for vision, that part of the brain will not function.

e. _____ When I was a child, I spent most of my free time with my grandparents. Since I was their only grandchild, they loved to entertain and spoil me.

Introductions

Once you have brainstormed some ideas, work on the introduction to your analysis paper. The purpose of an introductory paragraph is to get the readers' attention so that they will want to read on. The introduction begins with an _interest-catcher._ After the interest-catcher, you can give a little background information to help the readers understand the topic, but this is not always necessary. Finally, state your main point, or your thesis.

Preparing to Write 3: Writing Introductions and Conclusions

Introduction

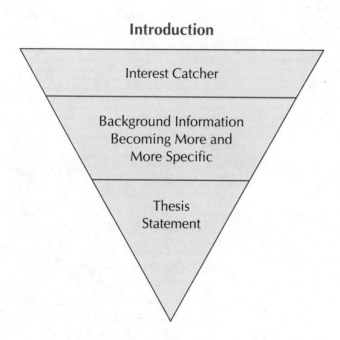

Interest Catcher

Background Information Becoming More and More Specific

Thesis Statement

ANSWER KEY

1. *Match these common, interest-catcher techniques for getting readers' attention. Complete the first column with items from the list. More than one technique may be used in each example.*

surprising fact   question   description of a scene

representative case   relevant quotation

Interest-Catcher Techniques	Examples
a. *representative case*	According to Toshitaka Nomi, blood type can determine how well two people can get along. Mika Matsui agrees. She found that her last boyfriend, a Type O, was too demanding. Type A's seem boring to her. Type B's don't like her, so she is looking for a Type AB.
b. _____	Recent studies show that multicultural groups perform better on tasks demanding creativity and strong organization.
c. _____	Having come from a small and conservative town, I had never seen anything as exciting as New York City. There I was, with my three new friends, in a city where anything could happen! We walked the streets, looking at every window and making plans to come back when we had more money. At night, in our dormitory, we would share what was in our hearts. I look back at it now as one of the happiest times of my life.
d. _____	What is the best way to make your relationship last? Say "Yes, dear," and go along with what your wife wants. Such is the finding of a new study by University of Washington psychologist John Gottman.

Interest-Catcher Techniques	Examples
e. _____ _____	As the old saying goes, "It's written in the stars." Each person's fate can be determined by the study of astrology.

2. *Go back to your quickwriting. What is the main idea that you want to express? Write an introduction here.*

_____

_____

3. *What kind of support do you need to provide for your main idea? Write your ideas here.*

_____

_____

Conclusions

Students often get stuck at the end of a composition. Writing conclusions can be as difficult as writing introductions. The purpose of the concluding paragraph is to give your paper a sense of completeness. Here are some techniques for writing conclusions.

- Restate your thesis. Use different words than you used in the introduction.
- Summarize the main points you made in the body of the paper.
- Predict what will happen if the situation continues.
- Suggest a solution to the problem.
- Include a significant quotation.
- Reuse the same technique you used in the introduction. For example, if you described a representative case or scene in the introduction, return to that case or scene.

4. *Now write a conclusion.*

_____

_____

_____

Now write your paper on the topic you have chosen. Be sure to include an introduction, support for your ideas, and a conclusion.

Writing an Analysis

Editing and Rewriting

More Editing for Articles

(ANSWER KEY)

*Review the editing rules for articles on pages 56–57. Then fill in the articles **a**, **an**, or **the** where necessary in the following passage.*

_____ researchers have found that _____ children who do not
  (a)   (b)

receive _____ attention as _____ babies do not develop in _____
         (c)   (d)   (e)

same way as _____ other children. This is because children's brains
             (f)

need _____ stimulation in order to develop. If _____ child is
      (g)   (h)

deprived of attention and stimulation, he or she may suffer from

_____ learning disabilities or _____ serious difficulties with
  (i)   (j)

_____ linguistic, physical, and emotional development. However,
  (k)

there is _____ hope for _____ these children if they receive
          (l)   (m)

_____ intensive care from _____ therapists, doctors, and parents.
  (n)   (o)

With _____ great deal of _____ work and _____ attention to
      (p)   (q)   (r)

building _____ skills that should have been learned as _____
          (s)   (t)

infant, _____ child with _____ severe problems may learn to
         (u)   (v)

function more normally.

Editing Checklist

Check the Content

1. *Exchange your analysis paper with a classmate. After you read your classmate's work, answer these questions:*

   ❏ Can you tell clearly what point the writer is trying to make?
   ❏ Is there an interest-catching introduction?
   ❏ Does the writer include enough support for the main idea?
   ❏ Is there a conclusion?

Check the Details

2. *Read your own writing again. If necessary, revise. Add or change details. Then continue checking your paper. Use these questions:*

❏ Are all your sentences complete?
❏ Did you use transitions and repetition expressions to connect ideas?
❏ Check your verb forms for correct subject-verb agreement and tense.
❏ Is the punctuation correct?

3. *Revise your writing.*

Vocabulary Log

What words or phrases would you like to remember from this chapter? Write five to ten items in your notebook.

Grammar and Punctuation Review

Look over your writing from this chapter. What changes did you need to make in grammar and punctuation? Write them in your notebook. Review them before the next writing assignment.

4 Surfing the Web

The fastest growing technology today is the Internet, an enormous worldwide network of computers that are connected by telecommunications. In this unit you will read and write about uses of the Internet.

These are some of the activities you will do in this unit:

- Read a description of the Internet and information about marketing on the Web
- Read Internet user data
- Read about romance via the Internet
- Complete a narrative
- Read the pros and cons of free speech on the Internet
- Write an argumentative paper

Chapter 9

The Internet

Do you have experience surfing the Web? Have you used the Internet? This chapter will introduce you to the basics of the Internet.

Starting Point

Discussion

People use computers in a lot of different ways both at work and at home. Which of the following computer uses are you familiar with?

Discuss the following with classmates and check (✓) your degree of familiarity.

	LEVEL OF FAMILIARITY		
	Have seen it	Can use it	Can teach someone to use it
HOME APPLICATIONS			
word processing			
scheduling			
recipes			
money management			
games			
THE INTERNET			
e-mail			
visiting Web sites			
OFFICE APPLICATIONS			
word processing			
spreadsheets			
databases			

Reading 1

Surfing the Web

People use computers to access the Internet. This article tells you more about the Internet.

1. *Read the article below.*

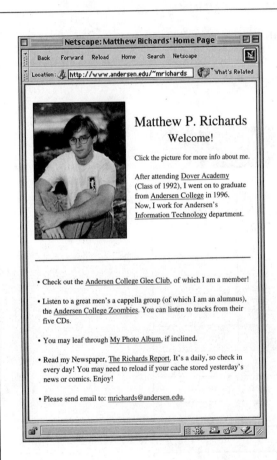

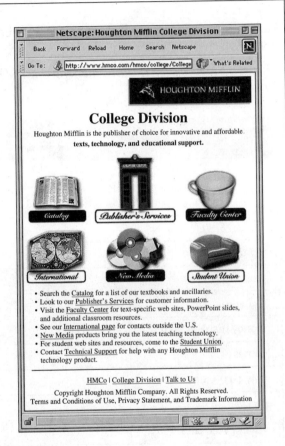

Surfing the Web

Having trouble understanding all of the excitement about the Internet? Here are some of the basics you will need to know. The Internet, millions of computers connected around the world by telephone lines, is the fastest growing technology today. The software that allows us to present and read information throughout the Internet is called the World Wide Web (WWW) or, more commonly, the Web. You've probably heard people use these terms interchangeably: "on the Internet," "on the Web." With navigational software, or browsers, users are able to jump around, reading here and there throughout the world. All of this browsing of the Internet is called "surfing the Web."

Each web site consists of "home pages," starting points for the Web user. These home pages are top-level documents, like the title page for the information they hold. They are written in hypertext mark-up language (html), which means they contain links to other web sites around the world. When you see a link, you click on it with your mouse, and that new web site is sent to your home computer. Anyone with a computer can make a home page and can create these links to other home pages or web sites.

Users may get information from a web site in different forms: text, graphics, video, or audio. They can connect to stores, libraries, and other people's lives, reading the home page that individuals, schools, companies, and organizations create.

Just as homes have addresses, each computer site has a Uniform Resource Locator (URL) address. If you know the address you want to go to, you don't need to browse. You just need to type the address in the locator box. The URL addresses usually have the following format: http://hostaddress/directory/filename. The host address will identify the computer that is connected to the network, the organization or school, and the domain (a group of computers that share the same common suffix). These are some typical domain suffixes:

.edu   education
.com   commerce
.org   organization
.gov   government agency

For example, *http://weber.u.washington.edu* is the site of the University of Washington. The first part of the host address tells us that the host computer is Weber. Then the University of Washington is identified. The last part of the host address is the domain, *edu*, for education. If there are more parts to the URL, they will take you to different parts of the university. For example, this address would take you to the ESL Programs' home page at the University of Washington: *http://weber.u.washington.edu/~eslinfo.*

Because of the growth in the number of companies with web sites, there are now more specific alternatives to using the domain suffix .com: *.firm* (for business), *.store* (for retailers), and *.arts* (for cultural organizations). Knowing the parts of a URL address is very important because you will need to evaluate the point of view of the web pages you read. The address tells you if you are reading factual information from an authority, the opinion of a private citizen, or the sales pitch of a retailer.

Besides getting information from the Internet, users are able to communicate with each other. They can belong to newsgroups, lists, or bulletin boards, and they can send one-on-one messages. This means they can read information as well as "chat" with other users around the world. The Internet has become an easy way for people to make friends and find companions. Its advantages are the incredible speed and the affordability of this kind of communication.

Many businesses are finding that the Internet is an inexpensive communication tool. If you want to find new customers, present a high-tech image for your company, provide fast customer service at a low price, then it's time to create a home page for your business. The Internet provides fast service much cheaper than faxing or overnight mail service.

In recent years, "anti-company" web sites have sprung up on the Internet. People who are dissatisfied with a company can create their own home pages with their own information about a company. For example, there is a web site called "Untied," created by people who were dissatisfied with United Airlines. Anti-company home pages are usually linked to discussion groups where other net users can add their comments. Rumors about companies can spread very quickly on the Web. For example, one baby food company has been flooded with mail for years because of an Internet story, a rumor that if you had a baby born in a certain year, you were entitled to hundreds of dollars in refunds from the company.

As with all new technology, the Internet also has a dark side. There is a great deal of concern about adult topics, such as pornography, which are available to children on the Internet. There is also an on-going debate about the freedom to say whatever you want to say on your home page. As this technology continues to develop, more exciting possibilities will emerge and, with them, debates over the benefits and harm to our society.

GUIDELINES FOR CREATING COMPANY WEB SITES

1. Read customer newsgroups to find out what people like and dislike about your products and the products of your competition. Find out what the FAQs (frequently asked questions) are.

2. Research on-line services, such as America Online, which your company can afford to belong to.

3. Make your home page very user-friendly. Remember that if you have a lot of text, it will be hard to read. Also, if you have large graphics, it will take the user a long time to down-load the file to his or her computer.

4. Make your home page navigationally clear—easy to move around in. Consider a simple page layout. Have a title bar at the top so users can move around to other home pages easily. Include an index or map for them to click on to move to other parts of your site.

5. Give some background of the company, such as outstanding accomplishments or a little history.

6. Hook up your home page to an on-line shopping mall or an electronic magazine.

7. Include a "what's new" section for your new products or services.

8. Have a link to "how to order" on each page of products.

9. Keep the customer at your site. Make your site engaging. Don't provide links to other competing sites.

10. Make sure the customer can easily link to Customer Service: FAQs, ordering, product support, telephone numbers.

2. *As you have seen in previous chapters, you can often figure out the meaning of a word from its context. Writers often give* **context clues** *to help you understand unfamiliar vocabulary. Here are some techniques to give context clues:*

- comma (,) before a meaning
- "or"

- dash (—) before a meaning
- example

- definition ("is called")

*Find words or expressions in the article with similar meanings to the words listed here. Underline the words or expressions—**the context clues**—in the reading that gave you the answer. Also note which of the techniques listed on page 110 for giving the meaning in context was used.*

	Meaning	*Context clues*
the Internet (paragraph 1)	millions of computers connected by telephone lines	comma
WWW		
surfing the Web		
home pages		
html		
URL address (paragraph 4)		
domain		
FAQs (guideline 1)		
America Online (guideline 2)		
user-friendly (guideline 3)		
navigationally clear (guideline 4)		

3. Apply information from the article to match these URL addresses with their sites. Write the number of the Web site in the blank on the left.

URL Address	**Web Site**
a. _____ http://www.royal.gov.uk	**1.** Santa Claus's interactive Web site
b. _____ http://www.thecanyon.com	**2.** The Mercedes Benz Club of America
c. _____ http://www.microsoft.com	**3.** the British monarchy's Web site
d. _____ http://north.pole.org/santa/ talk_to_santa.html	**4.** *The New York Times*
e. _____ http://www.metmuseum.org	**5.** Grand Canyon National Park
f. _____ http://www.nytimes.com	**6.** Microsoft Corporation
g. _____ http://www.mbca.org	**7.** The Metropolitan Museum of Art

Reading 2

Internet Users Worldwide

Being able to interpret charts and graphs is an important reading skill.

1. *Read the following report.*

READING TIP

Be sure to look at the titles, labels, legends or keys, and the size of the units when you begin to read a graph or table.

Internet Users Worldwide

Statistics from 1990 through 2000 illustrate typical patterns in the spread of a new technology, the Internet. In 1991, 80% of Internet users were in the US, where the technology was developed. This percentage dropped to 65% in 1994 as more and more people worldwide gained the technology to access the Internet. In fact, the fastest-growing group of people online today are those who do not access the Internet in English.

Table 1

1997 Rank	Country	Internet Users in Thousands	% Share of Total
1	USA	54,675	54.70
2	Japan	7,965	7.97
3	United Kingdom	5,828	5.83
4	Canada	4,325	4.33
5	Germany	4,064	4.07
6	Australia	3,347	3.35
7	Netherlands	1,386	1.39
8	Sweden	1,311	1.31
9	Finland	1,250	1.25
10	France	1,175	1.17
11	Norway	1,007	1.01
12	Spain	920	0.92
13	Brazil	861	0.86
14	Italy	841	0.84
15	Switzerland	767	0.77

Top 15 Countries in Internet Usage
(business, educational, and home Internet users)

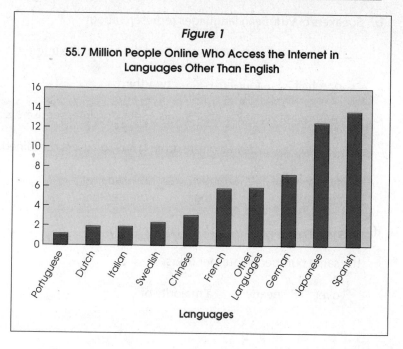

Figure 1

55.7 Million People Online Who Access the Internet in Languages Other Than English

ANSWER KEY

2. *Using the information in the introduction and Table 1, decide if these statements are true (T) or false (F) as you* **interpret the data.**

a. _____ We can conclude that the United States' share of the Internet market has increased more than 11% since 1994.

b. _____ Slightly over 75% of the top 15 countries had over 1 million users.

c. _____ With the exception of Japan, the top four countries were English-speaking countries.

d. _____ In 1997, the United States had more than two-thirds of Internet users worldwide.

e. _____ All of the Scandinavian countries had a minimum of 1million Internet users at that time.

f. _____ The combined number of non-European Internet users was marginally more than 70%.

3. *Using the information in Figure 1, fill in the blanks to* **interpret data.**

ANSWER KEY

a. Figure 1 shows that there are almost four times as many Japanese speakers on the Internet as there are _____ speakers.

    German   French   Chinese

b. Speakers of European languages represent about

_____ of the non-English users of the Internet.

    one-half   four-fifths   two-thirds

c. The number of Japanese and Spanish-speaking Internet users is

_____ all of the other language users combined.

    nearly equal   slightly   marginally
    to that of   less than   greater than

d. The Netherlands, Italy, and Sweden have _____ the same number of Internet users.

    over   nearly   a majority of

e. There is _____ 20 percent difference between

the languages with the greatest and the smallest number of users.

close to a   slightly over a   more than a

Reflect on Reading

In exercises 2 and 3 above, you **interpreted data**. When you interpret data, you provide a greater understanding of it than just repeating the numbers in the graph or table. Which sentence shows interpretation of data?

_____ There are 12.3 million Japanese and 3.1 million Chinese Internet users.

_____ Japanese speakers have almost four times the number of Internet users that Chinese speakers do.

Targeting

Internet Expressions

(ANSWER KEY)

· ·

With new technology, there are always new terms to learn. Below are some common expressions that you will hear when people talk about the Internet.

1. *In each lettered item, cross out the word that does not belong. Then write the topic of the words on the line. Use the topics in the list below. Refer to "Surfing the Web" on pages 108–110 if you don't remember the meanings of these words.*

Topics

verbs that describe looking for information on the Internet

being connected to the Internet

companies that offer Internet connection service

ways to describe "the Internet"

ways Internet users can communicate with each other

what you can find on a home page

a. navigate   browse   surf   ~~logoff~~   search

  verbs that describe looking for information on the Internet

b. newsgroup   bulletin board   e-mail   computer   chat room

  _____

c. hooked up to	on-line	logged on to	off-line	on

___

d. the Web	word processing	the Internet	WWW	the Information Super-highway

___

e. users	providers	on-line services	America Online

___

f. FAQs	links	http://	modems	URLs

___

2. As you read in chapter 1 on pages 5–7, collocations are words that commonly go together. In each set of phrases, circle the correct **collocation** for talking about computers and the Internet.

a. 1. log in the Internet
   2. log on the Internet

b. 1. get on the Internet
   2. climb on the Internet

c. 1. leave the Internet
   2. get off the Internet

d. 1. be on-line
   2. be in-line

e. 1. e-mail to someone
   2. e-mail someone

f. 1. construct an e-mail message
   2. compose an e-mail message

g. 1. send e-mail someone
   2. send an e-mail to someone

h. 1. spend time on the Internet
   2. do time on the Internet

i. 1. sign up for a discussion group
   2. participate in a discussion group

j. 1. subscribe a list
   2. subscribe to a list

Quickwriting

Have you been on the Internet? What was your experience? What are your favorite sites?

OR

Do you feel there is too much interest in the Information Superhighway?

Write in your notebook for ten minutes about your experience or opinion of the Internet.

Vocabulary Log

What words or phrases would you like to remember from this chapter? Write five to ten items in your notebook.

Class Activity   An Internet Search

Since anyone can write a home page, it is sometimes difficult to trust the information you read on the Internet. In this activity you will learn how to evaluate what is good, reliable information.

1 Choose a topic that everyone would like to do a Web search on. Then do a search on the topic, using a Web browser.

2 Select three home pages on this topic and answer these questions to help you evaluate the authority of the sites.

a. Look at the URL. What kind of site is this: business, government, or university?

b. What is the purpose of the site? Is this biased or unbiased information? How do you know?

c. Who wrote or sponsored the site? (This is often at the bottom of the home page.)

d. Is there any way to tell if this author is knowledgeable about the topic? For example, has the person written books on the topic? Is it a government agency or an academic institution?

e. When was this home page published? Is the information current?

f. In summary, do you think this is a reliable source on the topic?

Chapter 10

Romance in Cyberspace

In this chapter you will read about meeting people through the Internet and will write a narrative.

Starting Point

Pros and Cons of Internet Romance

The Internet is introducing people and helping romance grow. It's quite common these days to find people who met on the Internet, communicated as friends, then exchanged romantic e-mail messages, and eventually got married.

1. *Discuss these questions with a classmate.*

    a. What do you think are the advantages to meeting people via the Internet rather than in "real time," or face-to-face?

    b. What are the disadvantages?

2. *Share your ideas with the rest of the class.*

Reading 1

Cyberdating

People are meeting on-line, falling in love, and getting married. This reading will explain how this courtship often works and what to keep in mind if you enter into an on-line relationship.

1. *Read the following selection.*

Cyberdating

[1]   It's possible these days for people to fall in love sight unseen—though not unknown. Daily, tens of thousands of people spend hours at computers hooked up to the Internet in pursuit of love. Many applaud the ease of intimacy in this high-tech version of courtship, and some turn their on-line connections into off-line, real-life relationships.

[2]   Brandi Chionsini, 23, of Houston, met her fiancé, Jim Gavigan, 26, of Memphis in a "chat room" last March in her first hour of socializing on the Net. They plan to marry in December. "It's like we're two lost souls who found each other," says Chionsini. How do people on the Internet get to know each other? With a personal computer linked to a modem, plus a subscription to an on-line service, it's simple to have an active

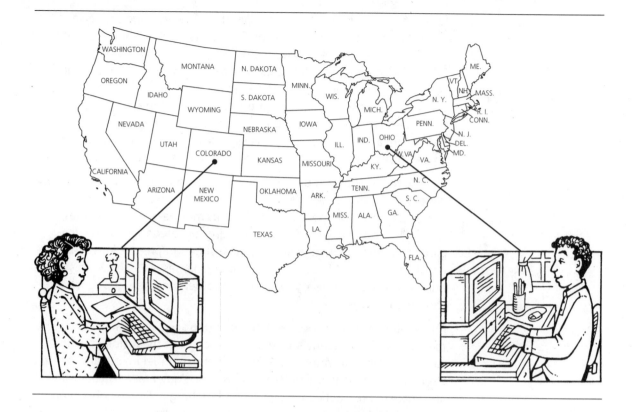

social life, albeit a virtual, not face-to-face, one. Each commercial service provider offers its own opportunities for members' interaction and also provides access to the World Wide Web, with its own communication options.

[3]   One striking difference between meeting people on-line and in real life is the anonymity of cyberspace. Members sign on with screen names that shield their identities and decide how much to reveal or whether to project new sides of themselves. A usually shy person can try out a more flamboyant personality. Such self-exploration can have positive results, says Sherry Turkle, a clinical psychologist and author. "A person can grow into the person they present. That piece of self that's inhibited can grow into something full."

[4]   Anonymity also can breed deception, of course. On-line, you can't be sure if the person describing himself as a 42-year-old basketball-star-turned-architect is really an 18-year-old student or, worse, a dangerous con artist. On the Internet, as in real life, it's essential to avoid giving out your real name, address, and phone number until you've known someone for a while. Another rule of the real world applies, too: Treat everyone you encounter with respect.

[5] A chat room is like a parlor designed for freewheeling conversation—except that there's no parlor. Each on-line service operates differently, but usually there are two to fifty people present at once. You follow the chatter—which appears like a script, with screen names and comments—on your screen. You can join in by typing remarks, which show up on everyone's screen almost instantly. At times it seems as though everyone is talking at once. But, unlike real life, it's never impossible to get a word in. Some people say it takes them time to find their "cybervoices," and they prefer to remain quietly at the edges.

[6] The flavor of the group discussion varies—from serious dialogues on issues to friendly queries ("Where y'all from?") to sexually suggestive talk—depending on the room. Chat rooms may be geared to singles, special interests such as astrology or biking, or categories such as religious denominations, gays and lesbians, or geographic regions. Participants enter and exit freely, and their screen names are listed. With some quick clicks of the mouse, you can access other members' (optional) short biographies.

[7] Another mouse maneuver enables you to send someone a private message, which instantly appears on the screen of the recipient, who can also respond privately. It's as though one member invites another to step out of the room and into the hallway for a quiet talk. "The hallways are where the real action is," says Alan Luxenberg of Philadelphia, who met Jan Norman when she sent him a private message from her computer at home near Boston. They're married now.

[8] For some, entering a chat room feels like arriving at a party they'd rather not attend. These are some on-line alternatives to meeting people:

- *Bulletin boards*—as varied in subject matter as chat rooms, but not "live". At any time you can post messages or respond to someone else's.

- *Personal ads*—you respond to other people's ads or create your own. Usually accompanied by photographs.

- *Newsgroups*—you post articles and opinions on a specific topic.

- *Your own home page*—your personal "address" on the World Wide Web.

[9] After a virtual connection is made, notes, love poetry, photos, even virtual flowers can be sent via e-mail. Then, for many who develop feelings for someone on-line, a major dilemma arises: whether to have a face-to-face encounter. Will the passion carry over into real life? Will the person they've gotten to know actually *be* the person as advertised?

[10] The accepted wisdom is that it's best for potential partners first to get to know one another through e-mail. Then, when they're comfortable, they can converse on the telephone and exchange photographs. If

they decide to meet, they should take the same precautions they would in meeting any stranger—getting together in a public place with other people around.

[11] "Maybe the computer was just incidental in our meeting," says Alan Luxenberg. "Maybe we would have hit it off just as well had we met some other way. But a person from Philadelphia and a person from Boston are not likely to just meet."

2. *Analyze these expressions in the* **context** *of the article and match the words with their definitions. Write the number in the blank on the left.*

ANSWER KEY

a. _____ "lost souls" [2]

b. _____ inhibited [3]

c. _____ flamboyant [3]

d. _____ anonymity [3, 4]

e. _____ con artist [4]

f. _____ deception [4]

g. _____ freewheeling [5]

h. _____ parlor [5]

1. an old-fashioned word for living room

2. a person who purposefully deceives others in order to get something from them

3. being dishonest

4. very bold colors or behavior; very noticeable

5. not able to do or say what you really feel

6. people who haven't found someone to be close to

7. not worrying about rules or correct behavior

8. the condition of not being named

3. *Read "Cyberdating" again to find this* **specific information**.

ANSWER KEY

a. Why do some people think cyberdating is great?

_____

b. Why does one psychologist believe this kind of self-exploration is healthy?

_____

c. What are the negative aspects of anonymity on the Internet?

_____

d. What are two important rules about meeting people on the Internet?

_____

e. What do you need to do to have a private chat with someone you meet in a chat room?

_____

f. What do you think it means to send someone "virtual flowers"?

_____

4. *A friend just sent you the e-mail message that follows. Don't look back at "Cyberdating." In your own words, write a short reply to your friend in which you **summarize the information** in the article. Use separate paper.*

> Thanks for sending me the get-well note. I'm getting better, but it's going to take a while before I will be out and around! In the meantime, a friend has suggested the Internet as something to keep me entertained. What do you know about using chat rooms?

Reading 2

Love at First Byte

READING TIP

Analyzing the sequencing of a reading is a critical thinking skill. If you can follow the order of events in a reading, it will help you understand and remember the content.

What is it like to fall in love in cyberspace? Here is a true story of two couples who met this way.

1. *As you read the following selection, look for clues to the **sequencing** of events.*

Love at First Byte

[1]   Mary and Lisa are good examples of Internet romance. These two young college students in Mississippi "met" two college men in California while they were playing a multi-user game on the Internet. In this game, much like in the real-life singles bar scene, players choose identities and wander around talking to real people in virtual time.

[2]   Lisa met her friend Dan, first, and talked about him constantly to Mary. Dan introduced his friend Evan, who began to have frequent on-line conversations with Lisa about Dan. He would ask her how she felt about Dan and tell her how much Dan liked her. Then Mary joined the

on-line conversations, talking to Evan to find out if Dan was really sincere. As it turned out, Mary and Evan had a lot in common. "We're easy-going, intelligent, sarcastic people who like to joke and enjoy the same kinds of things," said Mary.

[3] Soon Evan shared his phone number with Mary, but Mary felt she didn't know him well enough to share hers. One morning Mary and Lisa heard news of an earthquake in California and got scared. Mary phoned Evan to find out if he and Dan were okay. Evan asked for her number, called her back that night, and the two of them talked for ten hours!

[4] They phoned each other almost every night after that and exchanged pictures, and Evan frequently sent chocolates and flowers. Finally, Mary and Lisa flew from Mississippi to California to meet their on-line mystery men.

[5] Everybody was nervous. "None of us were sure how an Internet-and-phone relationship would transfer into real life," Lisa said.

2. *Write numbers in the blanks to show the sequence of events in "Love at First Byte."*

   a. _____ Dan met Lisa on the Internet while both were playing a multi-user game.

   b. _____ Evan gave his phone number to Mary.

   c. _____ Evan sent chocolates and flowers to Mary.

   d. _____ Lisa met Evan on the Internet after Dan introduced him to her.

   e. _____ Mary and Evan talked for ten hours on the phone.

   f. _____ Mary called Evan and Dan to hear if they were okay.

   g. _____ Mary and Lisa flew to California to spend a weekend with Evan and Dan.

   h. _____ Mary talked to Evan to find out if Dan was an honest guy.

   i. _____ There was an earthquake in California.

   j. _____ Mary shared her phone number with Evan.

3. *What do you think happened on that first "real-time" weekend together? Share your ideas with a classmate.*

4. *Reread the rules for cautiously meeting people on-line in "Cyberdating," pages 118–121. Were Mary and Lisa cautious about getting to know these men over the Internet? How? Discuss your ideas with a classmate.*

Targeting

Expressions for "Said"

When you are writing a narrative, you use quotation marks to indicate direct speech, and you periodically state who was speaking so that the reader does not get lost. However, you don't want to overuse "said."

Circle the best alternative to "said."

a. "You can get acquainted on the personality level first. You don't have to worry about what you look like or get distracted by sexual feeling," one man from Finland (exclaimed to, told) us.

b. "I realized how much we had in common!" Megan (argued, exclaimed). "We both love music and have traveled a lot."

c. "I know there is some danger involved, like some really weird guy or maniac but it's worth it," she (argued, wondered). "You could meet your soulmate on the Internet."

d. "Scary?" he (told her, wondered). "I don't think it's any scarier than walking up to a total stranger at a party and trying to start a conversation with her."

e. According to Dr. Dolan, first impressions matter on the Internet, just as they matter in real-life first encounters. "Be careful about your spelling and grammar," she (replied, suggested).

f. "No," George (wondered, replied), "I just don't believe that's true. I don't think carrying on a relationship on the Internet when you are a married man means you are being unfaithful to your wife." George absentmindedly ran his left thumb back and forth across his wedding ring. "I wouldn't actually be having an affair with another woman," he (told, advised) the group, "it's more like a fantasy, a harmless daydream."

g. "How honest should you be when you start a relationship with a stranger on the Internet?" (confided, wondered) Connie.

h. "Don't tell anyone, but it's a great way to flirt," (confided, advised) a woman in Cincinnati. "I have a ball doing it and I feel totally safe because I am in my home, nameless, and thousands of miles from that man."

i. "I once described myself as if I looked like a fashion model," Dorothy (wondered, admitted). "Lots of women do. And have you noticed the guys always describe themselves as if they all looked like Tom Cruise?"

j. "This is my advice: be honest and be realistic. The chance that the two of you could meet and really find each other as attractive in real time as on-line are pretty slim," David, a psychiatrist from Helena, (advised, exclaimed).

Writing

....

What happened once Lisa and Mary ("Love at First Byte") got off the plane in California?

Use your imagination to figure out what happened when Lisa and Mary ("Love at First Byte") got off the plane in California. What happened next in the story? Plan your narrative here.

Preparing to Write: Planning a Narrative

	Evan and Mary	*Dan and Lisa*
meeting at the airport/ Friday evening		
Saturday		
Sunday		
after that weekend		

WRITING TIP

A narrative will come alive for the reader if you use descriptive vocabulary and provide details for each scene.

Complete the story of these two young couples. Use quotation marks for direct speech and don't overuse "said." Sequence the story in chronological order.

Writing a Narrative

Editing and Rewriting

Editing for Punctuation with Quotes

If you are using quotes in a story, you must punctuate correctly; otherwise, the dialogue may be confusing to the reader.

1. *Study these rules.*

Rules	Examples
Begin the quotation with an opening quotation mark and end with a closing quotation mark. These marks will make it clear to the reader what the exact words are.	My dad always said, "Be yourself and people will love you." I have never forgotten his advice.
Each person's part in the dialogue is a new paragraph. Indent the line each time a new person speaks.	———>"Did you talk to him?" Mary asked. She had been waiting all day to ask Lisa. ———>"I couldn't get on the computer last night," Lisa replied.
Use a comma to introduce or interrupt a direct quotation. Begin the quoted sentence with a capital letter.	My dad always said, "Be yourself and people will love you." "Be yourself," my dad always said, "and people will love you." "Be yourself and people will love you," my dad always said.
Put exclamation marks (!) and question marks (?) inside the quotation marks if they belong with the sentence being quoted.	"Get out of here! Did you hear me?" she shouted.

2. *Rewrite the paragraphs on the next page, correcting the errors in punctuating quoted speech. Follow the rules for punctuating and indenting quoted speech.*

Evan and Dan were waiting for Lisa and Mary with flowers. When the young women came off the plane, the men recognized them easily because they had already exchanged pictures with each other. (a) When Lisa and Mary walked close, Evan and Dan shouted "Welcome ladies! (b) Mary said, "Nice to finally meet you guys"! (c) Lisa said to Evan I've really been nervous about finally meeting. (d) Evan responded "me, too." Evan thought that Lisa looked lovely and Dan had a first impression of Mary as a very upbeat woman.

(e) "How was your date today"? Mary asked Lisa when she entered the hotel room after her great day with Evan. Mary suddenly realized that Lisa looked disappointed and exhausted. (f) "Dan was very energetic, cheery, and a neat person on the Internet, Lisa said, but in real life, he is actually very shy and doesn't talk much."

(g) "Can you imagine? I was desperate to continue our conversation and he usually only answered yes or no"! (h) She sighed "I felt like I was meeting a different man and the WRONG man." (i) "If we all four spend some time together tomorrow" Mary suggested, "do you think that would help?"

(j) "Thanks. That's really nice of you, but I don't want to bother you.

(k) "The man I met on the Internet and the man I met in California are just not the same. But that won't stop me from trying to meet someone else! Look at how happy you are."

Editing Checklist

Check the Content

1. *Exchange your narrative with a classmate. After you read your classmate's narrative, answer these questions:*

   ❏ Are there enough details to make the story interesting?
   ❏ Are the events told in a logical sequence?
   ❏ Does the story sound complete?

Check the Details

2. *Now, reread your narrative. If necessary, revise your writing. Add more details. Then continue checking your own writing. Use these questions:*

   ❏ Are verb tenses correct?
   ❏ Did you use "said" too many times? If so, use some alternative words from Targeting: Expressions for "Said" on pages 124–125.
   ❏ Is dialogue punctuated correctly?

3. *Revise your writing.*

3. *Read what really happened to these two couples.*

The first weekend was very awkward. "It was tough to relate the voice and the words coming out of nowhere to this real, flesh-and-blood person in front of me," said Mary. "On one level, I wanted to hold him and be close because he was the person I'd fallen in love with. On another level, though, it felt like I was touching a complete stranger."

This strangeness disappeared, though, and for a year and a half both couples exchanged visits. Eventually Mary and Lisa moved to California. Today, Mary and Evan are happily married, and Lisa and Dan are living together. Both couples are the best of friends and live 20 minutes from each other.

Vocabulary Log

What words or phrases would you like to remember from this chapter? Write five to ten items in your notebook.

Grammar and Punctuation Review

Look over your writing from this chapter. What changes did you need to make in grammar and punctuation? Write them in your notebook. Review them before the next writing assignment.

Chapter 11

Free Speech on the Internet

Anyone can publish his or her opinion on the Internet, but does everyone have the right to? In this chapter you will read the pros and cons of free speech on the Internet and write an argumentative paper.

Starting Point

According to the philosopher John Stuart Mill, if we silence the opinions of people, we lose the opportunity to learn if we are in error or to strengthen understanding of what we know to be true.

The Value of Free Speech

With a classmate, discuss whether you agree or disagree with these statements. Put a check (✓) under your responses.

	Agree	Disagree
a. Without free speech, democracy cannot exist.		
b. There should be no restrictions on free speech.		
c. People have the right to publish pornography (sexually explicit material that is intended to excite).		
d. Companies should be allowed to express their opinions about their products even if the information is false.		
e. Burning the flag of your country is an expression of free speech and, therefore, should be permitted.		

Reading

The excitement and growth of the Internet continue to bring up questions about the basic right of free speech. The selection on the following page explains some of the basic issues involved.

Free Speech

1. **Preview** the following academic reading.

    Which of these topics are probably included in this selection?

    _____ a quote from the President of the United States

    _____ information about decisions made by the government

    _____ arguments for and against free speech on the Internet

    _____ the history of the development of the Internet

2. *Now read the selection.*

FREE SPEECH

Freedom of speech and democracy are often linked. Can democracy exist if even a few people are restricted from saying what they believe? The United States Constitution guarantees free speech. However, over the years, the Supreme Court has agreed to three types of limits to free speech. These restrictions protect people from the dangers of free speech.

Limits to Free Speech

The first limit to free speech protects people against libel. Libel means making false written statements about a person that damage that person's reputation.

The second limit protects the common standards of the community. This is a difficult area. The court must decide if free speech is damaging the happiness of most citizens. The damage may come from obscenity (sexually explicit behavior, language, or material) or from blasphemy (speaking disrespectfully about God). Laws against profanity, or using bad language, are another example of this limit.

The final area is protection against internal disorder and interference with the operation of government. When free speech means treason, an action such as planning to overthrow the government of the United States, citizens must be protected. If free speech results in failure to obey US laws, or in violence or other crimes, this third class of limits applies.

Attempts to Limit Free Speech on the Internet

The government has made many decisions about these restrictions over the years. It has limited free speech in newspapers and in public places. However, the debate about limiting free speech on the Internet is relatively new. If speech on the Internet is libelous, obscene, or treasonous, should the government protect the community by censoring the Internet? Futhermore, would the end of free speech on the Internet harm democracy?

In 1996, the United States Congress passed the "Communications Decency Act." This act was designed to limit children's access to indecent material on the Internet. However, in 1997 the U.S. Supreme Court struck down the law. The court said the law was unconstitutional: it limited speech for children, but it also limited speech for adults.

Opponents of the Communications Decency Act include many high-tech companies doing business connected with the Internet. The leaders of these companies criticized any regulation of the Internet. They said that legislation such as the Communications Decency Act could stifle the growth of a unique new medium. They argued that the Internet thrives, like democracy, on participation and diversity of thought. These company leaders also said that parents could use computer programs to monitor and restrict their children's access to objectionable materials on the Internet.

Nonetheless, many parents continue to demand restrictions on free speech on the Internet. They argue that the pornography and explicit conversations in chat rooms on the Internet damage the health of society. Although there is still widespread opposition to regulation of the Internet, a growing number of computer users agree that some degree of government regulation is necessary. They want the government to pass regulations to protect the privacy of the user and to limit the amount of pornography available to children. Most computer users indicate that they do not trust high-tech companies to provide foolproof solutions.

3. *Outlining* is one way to understand the organization of a reading. Reread "Free Speech" to complete this outline.

I.   Freedom of speech and democracy

    A.   If restricted, is democracy possible?

    B.   Constitution guarantees free speech

II. Limits to free speech to protect citizens

    A.   _____

    B.   _____

        1. _____

        2. _____

        3. _____

    C.   Internal disorder or interference with the operation of the government

        1. _____

        2. _____

III. Attempts to limit free speech on the Internet

    A.   Limitations on free speech from past legal decisions

        1. _____

        2. _____

    B.   Debate about limiting free speech on the Internet

        1. Communications Decency Act

            a. _____

            b. _____

        2. Opposition to regulation

            a. _____

            b. _____

            c. _____

        3. Parents' arguments

            a. _____

            b. _____

            c. _____

4. *Complete the table using **context clues** to understand the meanings of these words.*

Word or expression	Meaning	Clue
a. restrictions [1]	limits	reference before "these"
b. libel [2]		
c. obscenity [3]		
d. blasphemy		
e. profanity		
f. treason [4]		
g. struck down [6]		
h. legislation [7]		

ANSWER KEY

5. *Match these examples with the terms in exercise 4 above.*

a. _____ walking around without clothes in a public place

b. _____ using God's name when you are angry

c. _____ telling your country's secrets to another country

d. _____ using very bad or rough language

e. _____ publishing a letter that accuses someone of stealing

6. *In paragraph 7 of "Free Speech," find words with meanings that are similar to these expressions.*

a. people who oppose a policy or action _____

b. related to _____

c. limit or hold back _____

d. grows well _____

e. differences _____

f. a form of mass communication _____

g. watch, keep track of _____

h. limit _____

i. offensive, causing disapproval _____

7. *In paragraph 8, find words with meanings that are similar to the expressions listed below.*   ⬭ ANSWER KEY

    a. limits and regulation _____

    b. the treatment of sexual material in a way to excite _____

    c. very clear and openly expressed _____

    d. unable to go wrong _____

    e. rules, restrictions _____

8. *Discuss these questions about the free speech controversy.*

    a. Who was happy with the Supreme Court's decision to strike down the 1996 Communications Decency Act?

    b. What is essential for the Internet to thrive?

    c. What is another way to say *diversity of thought*?

    d. What two areas did most people in a recent poll feel the government should regulate?

    e. Do you think libraries should restrict viewing explicit material so that other people near the computer users do not feel uncomfortable? Explain.

    f. Do you think there can be a foolproof solution to this problem? Explain.

9. *The selection on the next page includes typical vocabulary in the free speech debate. Complete the words with the correct form.*

Patrons Responsible for Internet Behavior

Should access to the Internet in libraries be restri_____? (a)

Librarians have reached a conclusion that the Internet is beyond

regul_____. (b) If filtering software is used to

restri_____ (c) the material that patrons view on-line, it

will limi_____ (d) access to medical and important sex-

education material. Not wanting to be smut police, limi_____ (e)

patrons' use of the Internet, librarians are asking patrons to

regul_____ (f) their own behavior while using computers in the

library and asking parents to monitor their children when they surf on-line.

Libraries, which have a strong tradition of intellectual freedom, find

it objec_____ (g) to set up contr_____ (h) for

Internet use. Because computer screens are in public areas, many libraries

across the country are simply asking patrons to use good judgment or are

trying to prot_____ (i) patrons by throwing out users

who display sexually explicit material. Another approach has been

to install screens that block peripheral views. However, there is no

guar_____ (j) that children walking by the computers will

be prot_____ (k) from viewing harm_____ (l)

material. Another idea is to move computers to a more remote part of

the library; however, avoidance of exposure to objectionable material

would not be guar_____. (m)

Some libraries have restri_____ (n) access to the Internet

by requiring an orientation session before going on the Internet. Each library patron is advised about the rules of conduct and reminded of the

potentially damag_____ effect of exposing children
                           (o)

to smut. Other libraries have limit_____ on-line use to
                                              (p)

children over 18 unless they have a parent permission slip.

   Internet smut is in our libraries. All of this is new for everyone,

but smart, dedicated people are trying to make it work without

limit_____.
          (q)

10. *Imagine that "Free Speech" is material that you studied in a course. Look
at your outline in exercise 3. Then, on separate paper, answer this question from a test in this course. Do not look back at the reading.*
Test Question: Write a summary of the recent debate about free
speech.

Writing

Preparing to Write 1: Choosing a Position

Resolving the problem of smut and free speech on the Internet is not
easy. You are going to write a paper arguing for or against limiting free
speech on-line. The first step is to decide how you feel about this issue.
What do you think should be done?

1. *Discuss these five positions on the issue with a classmate. What are the
pros and cons of each position? If there is another point of view, write it
in the Position 6 box.*

Position	Pros	Cons
1. Do nothing to regulate the Internet. Keep it free from bureaucratic (government or on-line provider) control.		
2. Do not have government regulation. Allow the on-line providers to control content.		

Position	Pros	Cons
3. Provide tools (e.g., filtering programs) so that parents can control access.		
4. Pass legislation that requires parental warnings and rewards Web page creators who rate their material. Create penalties for people who stalk children on the Internet or display child pornography.		
5. Do nothing until we know what effect the Internet really does have on the public.		
6. *(Add your own point of view here.)*		

2. *Share the results of your discussion with the rest of the class.*

3. *Choose a position or a combination of positions that you would like to defend.*

My position on this issue:

_____

Reasons that I feel this way:

_____

_____

_____

4. *Look at the arguments of the opposing positions. How can you argue against each of them? List your counterarguments below.*

Arguments against my position	My counterarguments

Your next step is to plot the organization of your argument.

Preparing to Write 2: Planning an Argumentative Paper

1. *As you write your paper, you need to give the readers background information about the topic. Can you assume the readers know what the Internet is? What will they need to know about censorship on the Internet?*

<u>My introduction</u>

Background information

_____

_____

_____

Statement of my point of view

_____

_____

_____

2. *After your introduction, write a paragraph arguing your point of view step by step. What will be the main points of your argument? List them here.*

_____

_____

_____

_____

_____

3. *In the next paragraph, present the opposing positions and your counter-arguments. Which will you include? List them here.*

_____

_____

_____

4. *Finally, write your conclusion in a paragraph. Some ways to conclude are to summarize your main arguments in different words or to project into the future if this situation continues. Write your concluding ideas here.*

_____

_____

_____

_____

Writing an Argumentative Paper

Write an argumentative paper. Take a position on the problem of free speech on the Internet.

Editing and Rewriting

···

EDITING TIP

After you finish your paper, make a brief outline of your main points and their support. This will help you see if your argument is logical and well supported.

Editing Checklist

Check the Content

1. *Exchange your argumentative paper with a classmate. After you read your classmate's paper, answer these questions:*

   ❏ Is the writer's point of view clearly stated?
   ❏ Is there enough support for the writer's opinion?
   ❏ Are there counterarguments for the opposing points of view?

2. *Now, reread your argumentative paper. If necessary, revise your arguments.*

Check the Details

3. *Add or delete information. Then continue checking your own writing. Use these questions:*

   ❏ Did you use correct word forms?
   ❏ Are the verb tenses correct?
   ❏ Are the sentences complete?

4. *Rewrite your argumentative paper.*

Vocabulary Log

What words or phrases would you like to remember from this chapter? Write five to ten items in your notebook.

Grammar and Punctuation Review

Look over your writing from this chapter. What changes did you need to make in grammar and punctuation? Write them in your notebook. Review them before the next writing assignment.

5 Cityscapes

In the old days, city dwellers didn't have much to say about how their city looked. Many cities grew without plans. However, as we enter a new century, urban planners are looking at ways to make cities friendlier and more comfortable. People are also more involved in decisions about public art and zoning laws.

These are some of the activities you will do in this unit:

- Read an article, an editorial, and letters to the editor about controversial public art and architecture
- Write a letter to the editor expressing your opinion
- Read about problems in cities and "new urbanism"
- Write a proposal

Chapter 12
Artistic Interpretation

Public art is an integral part of many cities. However, it is often controversial.

Starting Point

Looking at Art and Architecture

Work with a classmate. Answer the questions about these photographs.

1. *Write two adjectives to describe each picture.*

Photo 1	Photo 2	Photo 3
_____	_____	_____
_____	_____	_____

2. *Discuss the examples of public art in exercise 1. Which examples do you like?*

3. *Which projects do you think were most controversial? Which seem most conventional?*

Reading 1

Mr. Rana's Nose

In this section you will read about a controversy in a neighborhood.

1. **Preview** *the article on the following page. Look at the title of the article and answer the questions. Do not read the whole article yet.*

   a. From the title, what do you think the "fight" is about? What is an "eyesore"?

   _____

   _____

   b. Can you make any guesses about the meaning of *snooty*?

   _____

   c. The author pokes fun at this particular controversy by using many words that refer to the nose or facial features. What reference(s) does she make to these in the title?

   _____

   READING TIP

   Some of the words in this reading are **slang**, or playful words often used for humor. Don't worry about words that are unfamiliar to you. Just keep reading for the general meaning.

2. *Now read the newspaper article.*

In a Snooty Art vs. Eyesore Fight, Only One Side Aims to Save Face?

Fred Thornhill/ © Toronto Sun

Gio Rana is so proud of his nose that he doesn't mind wiping it in public. The giant nose hangs outside Rana's Italian Restaurant on Queen St. in the Beaches and was a gift from artist Jan Walsh.

TORONTO — Pierre Nadeau complains that Joseph Rana's nose "is an ugly thing, big, very offensive." Like some of Mr. Rana's other neighbors, Mr. Nadeau wants the nose removed. Toronto's city government emphatically agrees.

The Rana nose is indeed big. It's four feet high and three feet wide, built for Mr. Rana by an artist friend out of plaster and canvas. The giant schnoz is mounted on the building where Mr. Rana lives and operates a restaurant, and appears to be bursting through the second-story wall.

"It's creative, it's art, it was intended to poke fun at my own big nose," Mr. Rana says.

"It's nothing to sneeze at," counters Peter Gordon, city solicitor, who contests the protuberance is illegal, for one because it juts out above a restaurant door on a quiet street where business signs are banned. "We're trying to minimize commercial use of what is already a very commercial area," he sniffs.

But in fighting the first complaint filed by the city, the restauranteur's lawyer, Michael Caroline, successfully argued that the nose wasn't designed to have commercial value. The artist, Jan Walsh, said that to suggest the sculpture has any commercial intent is "absurd" because it is inspired by Mr. Rana's nose, "the subject of much amusement."

So the city then charged Mr. Rana with infringing a bylaw, allowing a structure to "remain in a city boulevard," because the nose overhangs city property.

But before you could say Cyrano de Bergerac, the city withdrew that charge in favor of a more pointed one: The nose violates city bylaw 12519, section 35, by placing a "structure, to whit replica of a nose structure, which encroaches upon the street allowance… without first having obtained leave from the Committee on Works and Council." Mr. Rana, who has spent about 20,000 Canadian dollars ($17,153) defending his snout, must appear in Ontario provincial court Friday.

His attorney concedes that the nose may protrude into city airspace a foot or so, but says the property in question is only a parking lot.

"This smacks of a vendetta," Mr. Caroline snorts, adding, "You can't legislate good taste. It wouldn't be illegal for Mr. Rana or anyone else to paint their house purple with orange polka dots. If that's what they want…Surely there's a better use for taxpayers' money than fighting this nose."

ANSWER KEY

3. *Scan the article and find words that are related to noses.*

Paragraph 2   a slang term for nose   **a.** _____

Paragraph 4   to let out air from the nose and mouth suddenly   **b.** _____

to draw in air through the nose noisily   **c.** _____

Paragraph 7	a famous character in literature who had a big nose	d. _____
	an animal's nose	e. _____
Paragraph 9	to breathe violently through the nose	f. _____

4. *The author has fun with expressions related to the nose in this article, but what does she really mean? Consider the expressions in* **context**. *Match the expressions with their meanings. Write the number of the meaning on the line.*

ANSWER KEY

Expression

a. _____ It's nothing to sneeze at.

b. _____ . . . , he sniffs.

c. _____ Mr. Caroline snorts

Meaning

1. expresses anger

2. shouldn't be ignored

3. expresses doubt about an attitude

5. *Analyzing relationships is an important reading skill. Label which arguments are the city's (CITY) and which are Mr. Rana's counter-arguments (COUNTER).*

ANSWER KEY

a. _____ infringing a bylaw; allowing a structure to remain in a city boulevard

b. _____ city space is only a parking lot

c. _____ juts out above a restaurant door on a quiet street where business signs are banned

d. _____ structure encroaches upon the street allowance without first having obtained leave

e. _____ nose doesn't have commercial value

6. *Circle the number of the best choice to complete these statements about the article.*

   a. According to Mr. Rana, which of the following is NOT true?

      1. The nose is a way to make fun of his own nose.

      2. The nose is art.

      3. The nose was put up to make money.

      4. The nose was inspired by his own nose.

   b. When Mr. Rana's lawyer says, "It wouldn't be illegal . . . ," he's making the point that

      1. a purple and orange house would be more attractive.

      2. people want their tax money to be used this way.

      3. the city just wants to hurt Mr. Rana.

      4. some people have different opinions about art.

7. a. *The word* commercial *appears four times in the article, each time with a different noun. Write the four word pairs here.*

   _____   _____

   _____   _____

   b. *Match the word pairs above with these meanings. Write the numbers of the meaning next to the word pair above.*

      1. designed to make money

      2. a place legally okay to use for business purposes

      3. used as a business

      4. capable of making money

8. ***Analyzing*** *is an important critical thinking skill. In a small group, analyze the different sides of the nose sculpture issue. Fill in the chart on the next page as you discuss these considerations.*

	Reasons to allow nose sculpture	*Reasons to ban nose sculpture*
City codes		
Value of property if eyesore exists		
Individual freedom to express self		
Different ideas about what constitutes art		
The overall look of a neighborhood		

Quickwriting

Do you agree or disagree with the statement below? In your notebook, write for five to ten minutes about your ideas.

"Unusual architecture or art is always controversial, but unconventional styles often become accepted after people get used to them. It takes courage to be unconventional and to have a vision different from everyone else's. The public should not try to limit creativity by saying that there are appropriate and inappropriate places for unconventional art or architecture."

....

Reading 2

A Very Large Eyesore?

Modern architecture is often controversial, and the Bibliothèque Nationale de France is no exception. The next selection includes a newspaper editorial about this building and readers' responses to the editorial.

1. *Read the editorial page and letters to the editor on the following two pages.*

Photo © Michel Ginies/SIPA PRESS

A Very Large Eyesore?

The technology of knowledge is changing so fast that no one can say for sure what the libraries of the future will look like. One thing they had better *not* look like is the Bibliothèque Nationale de France, otherwise known as the Very Large Library.

The library was one of 12 grand architectural projects envisioned by the late French President François Mitterrand. And, like I. M. Pei's glass pyramid at the Louvre and the supermodern Institute of the Arab World, the library project has been the topic of much controversy. Many scholars said that the library would be unworkable. The result is no longer considered unworkable — it is simply ugly. With four chubby glass towers at the corners of a vast sunken courtyard that serves as reading room, it radiates an intense ugliness, dominating the neighborhood. The towers, each shaped like an L, are supposed to look like four open books, but they don't. What on earth went wrong here?

The search for an answer to this question goes well beyond French politics or French architecture. The initial winning design in 1987 proposed four taller towers of transparent glass. The towers would fill up gradually like a thermometer so that passersby could watch the library's massive holdings grow. However, researchers and library professionals pointed out that, impressive as this might appear from the outside, exposure to strong sunlight in the transparent towers would most certainly destroy the books. There was also the difficulty the vertical arrangement would create for library workers who would have to go up and down the towers every time a basement-dwelling scholar wanted something.

Rather than abandon the design, the architect made changes to respond to these complaints. He shortened the towers. He also doubled the thickness of the towers' glass and lined them on the inside with wood paneling. The wood looks beautiful from the inside and it protects the books, but the twinkling transparency of the tinted glass is gone; instead, what you see from the outside is a sooty grayish tan.

Stripped of beauty, the Very Large Library offers just one message to the landscape, that of gigantism: *Those guys sure do have a lot of books!* However, in the information age, it is just this idea — the idea that volume equals meaning — that no longer seems true.

Someone has to preserve what Harvard's Patrice Higonnet, a scholar of French history, calls "the weird book, the arcane book, the book no one else will have." However, the proper measure of that task was never volume alone. Anyone who has tried to find something in the great oceans of useless or repetitive knowledge on the Internet understands this. The important thing is not how much information you have; it's how you organize or catalogue it.

Dear Editor:

After hearing all the negative opinions expressed about the Bibliothèque Nationale de France, I was expecting the worst as I walked inside once it opened. What surprise I felt when I saw the interior! No expense has been spared in making this one of the loveliest public spaces in Paris.

I encourage others to judge for themselves. I think others will be surprised, as I was, at the fine design of this project. This project goes beyond simple functionality. Future generations will value President Mitterrand's far-sighted vision in creating this outstanding architectural project.

Sincerely yours,

Alain Meurot

Dear Editor:

The debate over the aesthetic value of the library means nothing to me. The library is a functional building; it does not have to be beautiful. This is why I am so angry at the cost of building the library.

$1.5 billion dollars for building costs with an additional $250 to $300 million per year in operating expenses is an exorbitant amount! Of all projects to spend so much money on, a library is the worst choice: No one will even need to enter a library in another ten years!

Sincerely yours,

Françoise Bouchet

Dear Editor:

Few people have mentioned the key difference between the old library in Paris and the new one: access.

In the old Rue de Richelieu library, only scholars were allowed to use the library. The Bibliothèque Nationale is actually two libraries, one for researchers and one for the general public.

What better use of public money could there be than allowing public access to the library? I applaud the decision to build the BNF.

Sincerely yours,

Gerard Du Pont

Dear Editor:

Public planners should consider the design process of the BNF as a classic example of decision-making gone wrong. Consider these fundamental decisions:

1. The site for the library is on a flood plain. The interior garden sits 21 feet beneath the normal level of the Seine.
2. The architect chosen for the project was totally inexperienced in projects of this size.
3. The architect designed a building to house books with a view, instead of giving the view to the people, who are relegated to the lower floors of the building.
4. Once the fundamental problem of storing books in bright sunlight was "discovered," the architect decided to put wooden shutters inside the glass towers rather than redesign the project.
5. The inner garden mentioned above was not your average, everyday landscaping project: a whole area of a forest in the country was transplanted, tree by tree, to this spot.

It is quite ironic that the planning for a project to hold the nation's intellectual collection involved such ignorant (or self-serving?) decision makers.

Sincerely yours,

Lisette Duchamp

ANSWER KEY

2. *Consider the underlined words in* **context**. *Circle the number of the best meaning.*

a. With four chubby glass towers at the corners of a vast sunken courtyard that serves as reading room, it <u>radiates</u> an intense ugliness, dominating the neighborhood.

    1. shines with   **2.** hides   **3.** shows clearly

b. There was also the difficulty the <u>vertical</u> arrangement would create for library workers who would have to go up and down the towers every time a basement-dwelling scholar wanted something.

    1. difficult   **2.** up and down   **3.** in a line

c. Rather than <u>abandon</u> the design, the architect made changes to respond to these complaints.

    1. change in some way   **2.** give up on   **3.** stop

d. The wood looks beautiful from the inside and it protects the books, but the twinkling <u>transparency</u> of the tinted glass is gone; instead, what you see from the outside is a sooty grayish tan.

    1. sparkle   **2.** shining through   **3.** ability to be seen

e. Stripped of beauty, the Very Large Library offers just one message to the landscape, that of <u>gigantism</u>: *Those guys sure do have a lot of books!*

    1. ugliness   **2.** hugeness   **3.** saying

f. The important thing is not how much information you have; it's how you organize or <u>catalogue</u> it.

    1. put in logical order   **2.** refer to   **3.** store

ANSWER KEY

3. *Answer the following questions about the editorial.*

a. In paragraph 1, does the editor hope the library of the future will or will not look like Paris's Very Large Library?

_____

b. According to the information in paragraph 2, which of the following are reasons that the editors feel the library is "simply ugly"?

_____ The towers do not look like what they were supposed to.

_____ It took a long time to build.

_____ It has a very bare appearance.

_____ It has four fat towers.

_____ It overpowers its surroundings.

_____ It doesn't work.

c. What were the library professionals' objections to the original plan?

_____

d. How did the architect change the plans to resolve the original objections?

_____

e. The editors feel the real failure is due to a much deeper problem regarding libraries today.

1. What is the deeper problem?

_____

2. What is more important: having a lot of information or finding the information that is needed?

_____

f. Circle the editors' **main point**.

1. There is too much information in libraries today. Libraries need to be more specialized.

2. The important thing about libraries is how they are organized, not their architecture.

3. The Very Large Library is a good example of how architecture has become weird in this century.

4. What some people think is art is an eyesore to others.

g. Although an editorial is a written opinion, it is usually based on some facts. Go back to the editorial "A Very Large Eyesore?" Write notes in the margins to show three facts and three opinions.

4. ***Analyze the points of view*** *presented in the Letters to the Editor. Briefly list the positive and negative comments.*

Positive Comments	Negative Comments
one of the loveliest public spaces in Paris	

Writing

Preparing to Write: Planning a Letter to the Editor

A letter to the editor is a personal response (opinion) to an article in a newspaper or magazine. If the newspaper or magazine decides to publish your letter, it will appear in the Editorial section of the newspaper or magazine.

1. *Read the information on the next page about the format and language of formal opinion letters such as letters to the editor.*

Letters to the editor should contain
- a reference to the original article, including the title of the article, author, and date
- your supported opinion
- a possible solution to the problem or the kind of problem

Since you are expressing your opinion, write the letter using "I."

Referring to the Author In the [date] article entitled "...," [author] says ... [author], in her [date] article on [subject], states ...	In **her article entitled "Snooty Art or Eyesore,"** **Suzanne McGee** pokes fun at the idea of a nose as public art.

Referring to the Article
Your [date] article on [topic] ...
   is an example of ...
   brings up the issue of ...
   describes/mentions ...
	Your **February 19 article** on the Bibliothèque Nationale **mentions** a number of important issues about the future of libraries.

Expressing Your Opinion I agree/disagree with [person/opinion] that ...	**I agree with** Mr. Rana's attorney that the city is acting vengefully in trying to get Mr. Rana to remove his nose.
Suggesting a Solution [person/organization] should ... I hope that ... It's my hope that ...	**The neighbors should** pay for the removal of the nose if they dislike it so much. **It is my hope that** an agreement can be reached on this issue.

2. *Imagine you are writing a letter to the editor about Mr. Rana's nose sculpture. Write a reference sentence to begin your letter.*

_____

_____

3. *Write your opinion of the Rana nose controversy.*

_____

_____

4. *Write your suggestion for resolving this problem and your hope for dealing with this kind of issue in the future.*

_____

_____

_____

Writing a Letter to the Editor

Write a letter to the editor arguing for or against Mr. Rana's nose sculpture.

OR

Choose an editorial in a local or national newspaper and write a letter to the editor arguing for or against the issue.

OR

Write a composition describing what you like or dislike about an unusual building or public sculpture.

WRITING TIP

Letters to the editor are sometimes humorous, but writers usually try to maintain a formal tone.

Editing and Rewriting

Editing for Sentence Variety

Good writing includes a variety of sentence types. Alternate simple sentences with more complex sentences.

1. *Study the sentence structures and examples on the next page.*

Sentence Structure	Examples
simple sentence S + V	The structure overpowers the neighborhood.
compound sentence S + V [and/or/but] S + V	The exterior is dramatic and the colors are bold.

complex sentence
   (conjunction) dependent clause, independent clause
OR
   independent clause (conjunction) dependent clause
	Because the towers are so ugly, it is an eyesore in the neighborhood.
	
	Neighbors have complained because the house does not fit in with the traditional community.
	
	If they had stricter zoning laws, this would not have happened.

compound/complex S + V [and/or/but] (conjunction) dependent clause, independent clause	Many people considered the sculpture to be art, but because it violated city code, it had to be taken down.
introductory phrase phrase, S + V	By painting the house purple, he was sure to anger the neighbors. Located in the suburbs, this high-rise building stands out like a sore thumb.

2. Look at your letter to the editor or your description of why you like or dislike a building or sculpture. Analyze your sentence structure. Tally (keep count of) how many of each kind of sentence you have by making a mark in the categories in the chart above.

3. If you have too many simple sentences, change some of them to the other sentence types.

Editing Checklist

Check the Content

1. *Exchange your letter to the editor or description of why you like or dislike a building or sculpture with a classmate. After you read your classmate's paper, answer these questions:*

   ❏ What point of view does the writing express?
   ❏ Are there enough details?

Check the Details

2. *Now, reread your letter or description. If necessary, revise your writing. Add more details if necessary. Then continue checking your own writing. Use these questions:*

   ❏ Do you have a reference to the original article, your opinion, and a hope for the future?
   ❏ Is your opinion supported?
   ❏ Have you used the past tense for events that happened in the past and the present tense for your current opinion?
   ❏ Have you been consistent in your use of verbs (tense and real or hypothetical perspective)?

3. *Rewrite your paper.*

Vocabulary Log

What words or phrases would you like to remember from this chapter? Write five to ten items in your notebook.

Grammar and Punctuation Review

Look over your writing from this chapter. What changes did you need to make in grammar and punctuation? Write them in your notebook. Review them before the next writing assignment.

Chapter 13

No Sense of Place

The unplanned development of many of our large cities has resulted in a hodgepodge—a messy mixture. In this chapter you will read about problems in city growth and write a proposal to revitalize a property in your town or city.

Starting Point

Comparing City Scenes

Most people live in cities or suburban areas today. These pictures show a typical suburban strip mall and a more traditional mixed-use neighborhood.

1. *With a partner, list the characteristics of each scene in the spaces provided on the next page.*

Suburban Strip Mall	Traditional Mixed-Use Neighborhood
buildings away from the street	houses close to the street
_____	_____
_____	_____
_____	_____
_____	_____

2. *Compare your list with your classmates' lists.*

3. *Do you live in an urban, suburban, or rural area? What is it like? What qualities make it an attractive or an unappealing place to live?*

Reading

No Sense of Place

READING TIP

Analyzing the patterns of a writer's arguments will help you understand the main points. In this selection, notice the many cause-and-effect relationships.

Changes in the appearances of towns and cities in America since the middle of the twentieth century have caused changes in the quality of life.

1. *Read the following selection.*

No Sense of Place

[1] Something is wrong with the places where we live today. Much of our environment has become suburban streets full of ugliness: miles and miles of cars, big-box stores, discount warehouses, and fast-food franchises. Gone are the quaint neighborhoods with their small-town friendliness. Because everything is too far away to walk to, the car dominates our lives. People must drive to restaurants, stores, public offices, and schools. As a result, there is a feeling of isolation, a lack of community, and no sense of place.

[2] In the decades following World War II, suburban areas were developed outside major cities. Before the war, the standard for new homes was very high. Homes were built well, using expensive building materials and styles. They were built to last for many decades. After the war, because houses usually consisted of modern, inexpensive building materials and styles, they did not connect us to the past. However, homes, schools, and shopping malls were also not built to connect us for gener-

ations to come. In fact, they had a short design life of fewer than 50 years. This throwaway philosophy continues today.

[3] Residences used to be an integral part of a neighborhood. The street was understood to be an outdoor room. Since homes and businesses looked onto the street, people could watch and participate in the life of the street. Today, for security and privacy reasons, contemporary homes and buildings are designed to separate us from that outdoor room.

[4] Another problem is zoning laws. Almost everywhere in the United States such laws prohibit building the kinds of places that Americans themselves consider authentic and traditional—the kinds of places they pay to visit when on vacation. Corner grocery stores can't exist in residential neighborhoods; homes can't be close together or close to tree-lined streets. Workplaces must be separate from residential areas. In addition, residential areas divide people by income, age, and even family size. What are the chances that a 20-year-old college student would live next to a high-income family of three or an elderly couple?

[5] Current zoning codes create areas of commercial sprawl, apartment complexes, and housing subdivisions as illustrated in this sketch. This kind of strict separation of our lives is markedly different from traditional neighborhood design, which is characterized by homes close to narrow streets and a mixture of residential, commercial, and public buildings.

CURRENT ZONING CODES

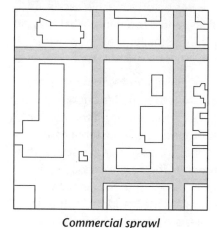

Commercial sprawl

TRADITIONAL NEIGHBORHOOD DESIGN

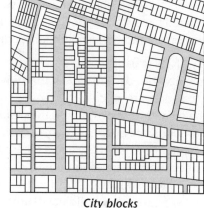

City blocks

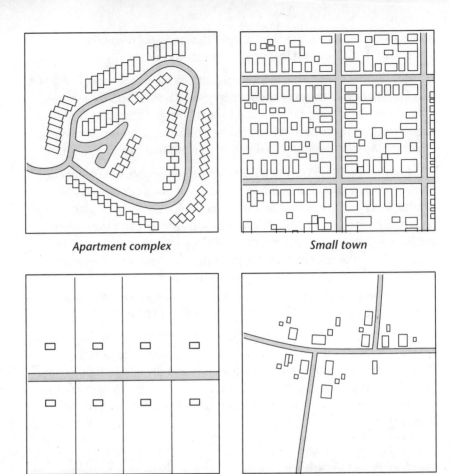

Apartment complex

Small town

Housing subdivision

Village

[6] This separation of areas makes us even more dependent on cars to carry out the business of our lives. This is design on a machine scale, rather than on a human scale. It is soul-less and depressing. What is needed to revitalize our cities and our lives is smaller-scale cities with clusters of traditional neighborhoods.

[7] "New urbanism" is a movement to refocus the development of city neighborhoods. The idea of this movement is to bring life back into urban areas by re-creating certain qualities of village life. In this concept, the basic unit of planning is the neighborhood, and a cluster of neighborhoods will be like a town. Each neighborhood is limited in size, with a well-defined boundary and a focused center. The neighborhood should not be more than a five-minute walk from the edge to the center and a ten-minute walk edge to edge. Human scale is the standard for the size and appearance of buildings. Automobiles are permitted, but they do not take precedence over human needs. For that reason, the neighborhood has a public-transit stop.

[8] The secondary units of planning are corridors and districts. Corridors can be parks, nature preserves, travel routes, railroad lines, or a combination of these. Districts are made up of streets where special activities take place. The French Quarter of New Orleans is a good example of a district. It is a whole neighborhood dedicated to entertainment, but it also contains housing, shops, and offices.

[9] The urban village is a mixed-use neighborhood. This means it provides housing for people with different incomes. It also has different functions: commercial as well as residential. Buildings are similar in size and in relation to the street. Forms of housing are mixed: apartments, duplexes, and single-family houses are in the same area, and apartments are permitted over stores.

[10] In neo-urbanism, the street is the most important form of public space. Buildings are arranged to use the street as an outer room. That means that they are close to the street and that their entrances are clear and inviting. Street patterns are in the more traditional grid pattern; cul-de-sacs (dead-end streets) are strongly discouraged.

[11] Civic buildings, such as town halls, churches, schools, libraries, and museums, are located in the center of the neighborhoods. This location shows their importance to the community and gives a focus to the neighborhood.

[12] Finally, although city planners will try to avoid the sameness of new developments, they may follow an architectural code. This will give some basic unity in the design of an area and create a sense of harmony. This focus on the way people will *feel* when they live in an area is a key difference between new urbanism and the old, uncontrolled development of cities.

2. *Match these adjectives with their noun equivalents. Write the number on the line.*

ANSWER KEY

a. _____ urban   **1.** suburb

b. _____ rural   **2.** city

c. _____ suburban   **3.** countryside

3. *Match each expression with its opposite. Write the number on the line.*

ANSWER KEY

a. _____ traditional   **1.** commercial

b. _____ residential   **2.** multi-family units

c. _____ single-family homes   **3.** contemporary

d. _____ public transit   **4.** restricted use

e. _____ mixed use   **5.** private transportation

4. *With a classmate, think of examples to explain what the author means by the following underlined phrases.*

a. The car <u>dominates</u> our lives.

We can't do anything without having a car because every-

thing is spread out. Parking lots, garages, and highways

take up a lot of space.

b. The result is a <u>lack of community</u> and <u>no sense of place</u>.

c. Gone are the <u>quaint neighborhoods</u> with their small-town friend-liness.

d. Houses had a <u>short design life</u> of fewer than 50 years.

e. This <u>throwaway philosophy</u> continues today.

f. The street was understood to be an <u>outdoor room</u>.

g. Another problem is <u>zoning laws</u>.

h. Current zoning codes create areas of <u>commercial sprawl</u>.

_____

_____

i. This is design on a <u>machine scale</u>, rather than on a human scale.

_____

_____

j. This is <u>soul-less</u> and depressing.

_____

_____

k. In this concept, the basic unit of planning is the neighborhood, and a <u>cluster</u> of neighborhoods will be like a town.

_____

_____

l. The secondary units of planning are <u>corridors</u> and districts.

_____

_____

m. Automobiles are permitted, but they do not <u>take precedence over</u> human needs.

_____

_____

n. Although city planners will try to avoid the sameness of new developments, they may follow an <u>architectural code</u>.

_____

_____

ANSWER KEY

5. *Complete these **cause-effect relationships** with information directly or indirectly stated in "No Sense of Place."*

Cause	Effect
Modern development	suburban streets full of ugliness
no quaint neighborhoods	
everything is far away	
	a feeling of isolation, a lack of community, no sense of place
modern, inexpensive building materials and styles	
homes and businesses looked onto the street	
	homes designed to separate us from the "outdoor room"
	commercial areas and residential areas separate
automobiles not permitted	
re-creating certain qualities of village life	

Reflect on Reading

Not everything you read is true, even if it may sound factual. Part of critical thinking is **distinguishing fact from opinion**. Distinguish fact from opinion in "No Sense of Place" by underlining three examples of the writer's bias (opinion). How does the writer organize the information to persuade the reader?

6. *Read the following report about proposals for the use of a piece of property in a suburban area. Which proposal follows the philosophy of new urbanism? Why? Which development would you prefer to live in? Draw a diagram of each plan and show its differences.*

The town planning board faced a difficult decision on Wednesday night as it met to consider two proposals for the 10 acre site of the old Cody farm. The Holly Farms Corporation proposes a development of twelve houses, each with an attached garage facing the street. Each house would be between 3000 and 3500 square feet. The plan calls for one road to wind through the development.

The Grant Co-Housing Group presented its plan for use of the land: a cluster of fifteen smaller dwellings (2400 square feet maximum) grouped around a central park-like area. To one side of the cluster would be a 4500 square foot common house. This common house would contain a central dining area with a kitchen as well as a playroom, library, and workshop. The plan requires that the planning board approve two variances to current zoning codes: the higher density of 1.5 residences per acre and the size limitation for the common house and two covered parking areas on two sides of the development. The co-housing group contends that the impact of these variances will be minimal since the houses will be grouped more closely together with walkways instead of roads going through the center of the development.

Local citizens spoke on both sides of the issue at the meeting. The planning board decided to postpone its decision until the town lawyer has had a chance to consider the co-housing proposal.

7. *Discuss these questions with a classmate.*

   a. How does the description of contemporary cities in "No Sense of Place" compare to city growth in your own culture?

   b. What characteristics does the new urbanism have that are similar to village life?

c. What is your opinion of the new urbanism? Is this kind of change in city life important? Is it possible to change city life? Will the new urbanism make a difference?

Targeting

....

The Language of Proposals

When writers create proposals, they usually follow a problem/solution format.

1. *Study these guidelines and examples.*

Guidelines	Examples
The description of the problem is often expressed with a noun clause or phrase.	The biggest problem is the **lack of zoning laws**. *(noun phrase)* The problem is **that no zoning laws exist**. *(noun clause)*
The description of the proposed solution is also often expressed with a noun clause or phrase.	We advise **immediate action**. *(noun phrase)* We advise **that they take immediate action**. *(noun clause)*
The noun clause that follows the proposal contains the simple form of the verb.	My proposal is that the city **establish** stricter zoning regulations. They proposed that plans for all new buildings **be** approved by a committee. It is important that the architect **submit** a design by the end of the month. I recommend that the neighborhood council **take** action immediately.

Guidelines	Examples
Use nouns, adjectives, and verbs to express the importance or urgency of your solution.	nouns: *advice, proposal, recommendation* adjectives: *advisable, essential, imperative, important, necessary, urgent, vital* verbs: *insist, propose, recommend, suggest, urge*
You can present options in a variety of ways.	There are two possible solutions to this problem: stricter regulations or an approval committee. There are several alternatives. One would be to make stricter regulations. Another would be to . . . The third possibility would be to . . .
The solution to the problem is usually hypothetical (not true yet), so the conditional may be used, particularly in presenting different options. However, using the simple future instead creates a stronger impression in a recommendation.	This approval process **would improve** the quality and design of new buildings. *(conditional)* This approval process **will improve** the quality and design of new buildings. *(simple future)*

2. *Read this description of a neighborhood with problems. Then complete the sentences.*

This used to be a quiet residential area, but now it is very busy. On all four corners of the intersection, there are small shopping centers with busy parking lots. Cars are turning in and out of the parking lots from all directions. There are no sidewalks, so children walking to stores have to walk in the street.

a. One problem is _____

b. Another problem is _____

c. Therefore, we suggest _____

d. We also advise _____

e. It is urgent _____

f. This solution _____

g. Everyone _____

Writing

Preparing to Write 1: Needs Analysis

You are going to write a proposal for revitalizing an abandoned piece of property or building. In a group, follow these steps to identify the needs of the various interest groups involved in the decision.

1. *Select a property or a building that you think could be used better. If possible, visit it as a group. Why does this place need to be revitalized? List the reasons.*

   _____

   _____

   _____

   _____

2. *What are the needs of the interest groups regarding the property or building you have chosen?*

Interest group	Needs
owner of property	*make more income*
users of property (old or proposed new users)	

Interest group	Needs
neighbors of the property	
neo-urbanists	

3. Brainstorm solutions for each problem in revitalizing this property. Analyze your possible solutions based on the needs of the interest groups in exercise 2.

Problem	Solution	Whose needs will this solution meet?

Preparing to Write 2: Preparing the Parts of a Proposal

A proposal usually has a title page, a table of contents, and sections with headings. Typical sections are Statement of the Problem, Proposed Solution, Background, and Conclusions.

1. *Read this sample student proposal to rebuild a property near a university.*

Proposal for Use of a Parking Lot in the University District

Submitted to
The University of Washington

Prepared by
Jung-Min Lee
March 2, 1999

Abstract

Because the University District is a mixed-use area, we are faced with the challenge of listening to the various voices that represent commercial, residential, and institutional needs. The aim of this proposal is to reconcile these needs. As a result, we suggest that the parking lot be used as a site for a new ESL Building.

Table of Contents

Proposal for the Use of a Parking Lot in the University District

Statement of the Problem

A parking lot, which can accommodate fifty cars, is located at the intersection of 15th Avenue NE and 42nd Street. The reason that this parking lot is centered in dispute recently is both economic and neo-urbanistic. First of all, this property has not been successful for the owner in terms of making a profit. Second, this parking lot doesn't have an attractive appearance, appropriate to its surroundings. Third, the ESL Department facilities at this university are greatly overcrowded and the department needs a new location closer to the main campus.

Proposed Solution

We propose that this property be developed to house the ESL Department. The ESL Building (provisional name) will be a two-story building and have a parking lot in the basement, an international restaurant, a lounge, and a theater on the first floor, and staff offices on the second floor. The parking lot in the basement will be sufficient and convenient for the needs of visitors, staff, and students. The restaurant and theater can be a place to share

3

international experiences of staff and students. The staff offices and lounge can promote camaraderie.

Background

From the beginning, this plan has been concerned with meeting the needs of commerce, residents, and neo-urbanism. Commercially, this building can add much to increase the profit margin and expand the reach of commercial influence. Residents can use the facility as a place where they can experience the diversity of the world. To be more concrete, they can enjoy eating international food and watching movies or performances by ESL students in the theater. These experiences will lead to an effort to understand different cultures. In addition, formation of a new cultural space can create a community gathering place, a cornerstone of neo-urbanism.

Conclusions

The establishment of the ESL Building on this property will provide the following benefits:

- more income for the owner of the property
- a more attractive appearance in harmony with the neighborhood
- a greater sense of community
- larger facilities for the growing ESL Department

4

2. With a partner answer these questions about the proposal for the use of a parking lot.

    a. What parts are included on the title page?

    b. Does the abstract give a brief description of the problem and solution?

    c. Is there a page number on the title page?

    d. Is the title of the proposal repeated at the top of the third page?

    e. Are the sections single- or double-spaced?

    f. Is the first sentence of each paragraph indented?

    g. What is the spacing between sections?

    h. How are the headings highlighted?

Writing a Proposal

Write your proposal for the use of the property you have chosen. Use headings to define the parts of the proposal.

> **WRITING TIP**
>
> Proposals should be in block style: double-space between sections and don't indent.

Editing and Rewriting

Editing for Problems in Problem-Solution Writing

1. Read these suggestions for editing your proposals or other problem-solution kinds of writing.

Suggestions	Examples
Check for consistency in any lists in your descriptions of the problem and the solution. (See Chapter 3 on page 33 to review editing for consistency.)	We see two serious problems: **the lack** of zoning and **the increase** in crime. (parallel noun phrases) These problems could be solved by **studying** the situation and **working** together to find a solution. (parallel gerunds)

Suggestions	Examples
	It doesn't matter whether the committee is made up of **professionals** or **residents**, but a mix of both would probably be best. *(parallel nouns)*
	You can either **act** now or **lose** the opportunity forever. *(parallel verb forms)*
Check the verbs in any noun clauses, especially those expressing importance or urgency. These verbs should be in the simple base form.	We propose that a committee **be** set up immediately to study the problem.
	We suggest that the university **create** a task force to study the problem.
Check for consistency in verbs: the tense and perspective (real or hypothetical). See Targeting: The Language of Proposals on pages 166–167.	The problem **is** that the area **has been** neglected for years. We **need** to take action immediately to stop further decay. *(present perspective)*
	This problem **would not have happened** if the city's finances **had been** better. *(past unreal conditional)*

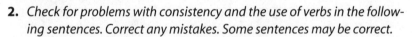

2. *Check for problems with consistency and the use of verbs in the following sentences. Correct any mistakes. Some sentences may be correct.*

ANSWER KEY

a. Building a gas station here would cause traffic congestion, safety problems, and pollute the ground.

b. This problem would never have happened if the city council had been doing its job and did not allow developers to build anything they wanted.

c. It doesn't matter whether the area is turned into a park or we decide to make a parking lot. Anything is better than what we have now!

d. I would have been a lot happier if the planners would have put something more modern there.

e. It needs a community effort and they clean up the area.

f. We strongly support an effort to add more residential housing in the area. We recommend that the city gives tax breaks to developers who invest in the area.

g. We have identified two solutions to the problem: making a park or build a walkway.

h. The city needs to get a committee together and makes a decision with input from the residents.

i. All the residents enter their houses from their garages. If people had to park farther from their houses, they would have more interaction with their neighbors. This interaction gives everyone more of a sense of community.

Editing Checklist

Check the Content

1. *Exchange your proposal with a classmate. After you read your classmate's proposal, answer these questions:*

   ❏ Does the proposal contain all the necessary parts?
   ❏ Is the plan easy to understand? Are the problems and solutions/benefits clear? If not, explain what you don't understand.

Check the Details

2. *Now, reread your proposal. If necessary, revise your proposal. Then continue checking your own writing. Use these questions:*

   ❏ Did you follow the suggested proposal format?
   ❏ Did you use the language of proposals correctly?
   ❏ Are items in any lists not consistent?
   ❏ Is the verb in the simple (base) form in a noun clause expressing importance or urgency?
   ❏ Are all sentences complete?
   ❏ Are the verb tenses appropriate?
   ❏ Are there any bare, singular count nouns? If so, cover them.

3. *Revise your writing.*

Vocabulary Log

What words or phrases would you like to remember from this chapter? Write five to ten items in your notebook.

Grammar and Punctuation Review

Look over your writing from this chapter. What changes did you need to make in grammar and punctuation? Write them in your notebook. Review them before the next writing assignment.

Class Activity   Pair Descriptions

Choose a place in your area to describe. With a classmate, visit that place and do the following tasks.

1 One of you write a description of the place from a positive point of view and one of you write a description from a negative point of view.

2 Exchange papers and see if you can help your classmate add even more details from a biased point of view.

3 Share your papers with your other classmates.

4 As an additional challenge, rewrite your description objectively, taking out the bias and opinions.

6 Closing the Loop: Recycling

Over the past few decades people have become aware of the problem of waste disposal. This unit focuses on the consumers' role in the recycling process and the controversy about recycling.

These are some of the activities you will do in this unit:

- Read about precycling
- Read a diagram and describe a scientific process
- Chart a scientific process
- Read the arguments for and against recycling
- Write an argumentative essay

Chapter 14

Shopping for Future Generations

Recycling paper is considered an environmentally sound way to reduce the use of natural resources, such as trees and cotton. In this chapter you will read about the process of recycling paper and describe a scientific process from a chart. You will also read about your role as a shopper in recycling.

The slogan "reduce, reuse, and recycle" reflects the need for conserving Earth's resources for the future.

What do you know about recycling? Answer these questions.

1. What products are usually recycled?

2. What opportunities do you have to recycle?

3. What has pushed us to recycle? Complete this list with a sentence describing each reason for recycling.

   landfill space _____*There is not enough landfill space.*_____

   raw materials _____

   energy _____

   population _____

4. "Precycling" means shopping in a way that will reduce the need for recycling. In a group, brainstorm ways to precycle. Then share your ideas with the class.

(ANSWER KEY)

Even before you recycle products, you can help conserve resources by precycling.

1. *Read what shoppers can do to reduce the amount of garbage.*

Shopping for Future Generations

As consumers, we are the most important link in the recycling industry. If we sort through our recyclable materials and make good selections when buying, we will help keep the cycle going. The first step is to precycle. Precycling means making a buying choice that will make recycling easier and reduce the amount of garbage we throw away. Here are some things you can do:

1. *Carry your own reusable shopping bag when you go shopping.*
2. *Buy in bulk—get a larger container of pop rather than a six pack. This cuts down on the cost of packaging.*
3. *Buy recycled paper packaging. If the unprinted side of a paper box is gray, not white, it's made from recycled material.*
4. *Avoid throwaway products. Examples are disposable plastic diapers, plastic razors, and non-refillable pens.*
5. *Avoid excess packaging, such as single helping packages.*
6. *Think recycling. Choose containers that you know can be recycled. Watch the wording. "Recyclable" is not the same as "recycled."*

The next step is to buy recycled materials. If we do this, we save on natural resources. We reduce the need to cut down trees or dig for oil or other minerals. Since it takes less energy to make recycled products, we save on energy. For example, recycled aluminum takes 95% less energy to make than new aluminum does. Manufacturing products from recycled materials creates less air and water pollution than making products from raw materials. We also save on landfill space, create jobs, and save money on waste management programs.

You will know if a product is made from recycled materials by its label. First, look for the recycle symbol:

If the product can be recycled, the recycle symbol is not filled in. If the product is made of some recycled material, the symbol is filled in with black, but the background is white. If the product is completely made from recovered material, the arrows are white on a black background.

Then read the label to see what percentage of "post-consumer" recycled material is in the product. Some products often made from recycled materials are paperboard, or lightweight cardboard boxes, such as those used in cereal, cracker, or shoe boxes. Plastic bottles used for household cleaners or shampoos may have recycled plastic in them. Look for at least 25% recycled content in glass bottles and jars, tin cans, molded pulp containers (egg cartons, fruit trays), bath and facial tissue, and paper towels. Aluminum beverage cans usually contain about 50% recycled aluminum. Envelopes, paper, and greeting cards also have recycled labels on them.

**Conserve our resources:
Reduce, Reuse, and Recycle!**

ANSWER KEY

2. *Determine what these labels say about the content of their products.*

---

3. *Now answer these questions about the brochure.*

a. Why are consumers the most important link in the recycling industry?

_____

b. What's the difference between *recyclable* and *recycled*?

_____

c. Why should you let store and restaurant owners know that you care about the environment?

_____

d. Why should we buy *recycled* products?

_____

Reflect on Reading

Authors usually have a **point of view** (their voice or bias) in their writing, which is often not explicitly stated. What is the point of view in "Shopping for Future Generations"? Why do you think the brochure was written?

4. *What do these recycling terms mean? Match the words with their definitions. Write the number of the definition on the line.*

a. _____ natural resources

b. _____ energy costs

c. _____ landfill space

d. _____ waste management

e. _____ garbage collection

1. picking up garbage at homes and businesses

2. the process of disposing of garbage

3. the expense of providing heat, light, fuel

4. coal, water, trees, minerals, oil

5. places where garbage is buried

Quickwriting

How conscious are you as a consumer? Are you buying recycled products? Are you precycling? What changes could you make in your shopping and lifestyle to help save the environment? Write for ten minutes in your notebook about this topic.

Reading 2

Paper Recycling

1. *What do you think happens when paper is recycled? With a classmate, **predict** the order that the paper recycling process follows. Write numbers to indicate the steps from 1 to 7.*

   _____ collect paper from recycling bins

   _____ make new paper

   _____ process paper into pulp

   _____ send to paper manufacturers

   _____ sort paper

   _____ throw paper away

   _____ throw recycled paper away

2. *Now quickly **skim** the article to check the order that you predicted.*

Paper Recycling

Recycled paper is an excellent example of how reusing products can result in expanded business opportunities. Recycling began in the early 1970s with the collection of corrugated boxes and old newspapers. The first 20 years were not at all profitable. In fact, too much paper was collected, prices fell, and this hurt the recycling programs in many cities. For a while, it seemed as though recycling was not going to be worth it.

However, by the early 1990s de-inking technology was developed, making a higher quality paper available from office wastepaper. Paper mills are now producing a wide variety of business supplies from recycled paper, and the markets for recycled paper are expanding. With such high demand, papermakers want guaranteed suppliers. Therefore, they are eager to sign long-term contracts with city recycle programs. The most important link in the cycle continues to be the consumer. We not only need to recycle household and office paper, we need to close the loop by buying recycled products.

Here is what happens to the paper you recycle.

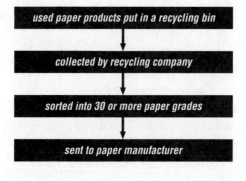

used paper products put in a recycling bin

↓

collected by recycling company

↓

sorted into 30 or more paper grades

↓

sent to paper manufacturer

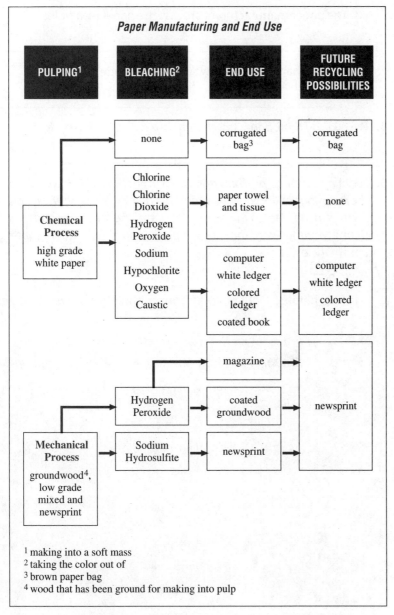

Paper Manufacturing and End Use

PULPING[1]	BLEACHING[2]	END USE	FUTURE RECYCLING POSSIBILITIES
	none	corrugated bag[3]	corrugated bag
Chemical Process high grade white paper	Chlorine Chlorine Dioxide Hydrogen Peroxide Sodium Hypochlorite Oxygen Caustic	paper towel and tissue	none
		computer white ledger colored ledger coated book	computer white ledger colored ledger
	Hydrogen Peroxide	magazine	newsprint
		coated groundwood	
Mechanical Process groundwood[4], low grade mixed and newsprint	Sodium Hydrosulfite	newsprint	

[1] making into a soft mass
[2] taking the color out of
[3] brown paper bag
[4] wood that has been ground for making into pulp

3. *Read the article more carefully and write about what happens after each of the following steps in the paper recycling process.*

ANSWER KEY

   a. The paper products are collected by a recycling company.

   _____

   b. The paper is sorted into different grades.

   _____

c. The paper manufacturers process the paper into pulp.

_____

d. The mechanical process works on low grade mixed paper.

_____

4. _Why do you think paper towels and tissues cannot be recycled?_

_____

5. _Learning common **prefixes and roots** in English will help you decode the meanings of unfamiliar words more quickly. What do the following prefixes mean? Match the prefix with one of the meanings and then think of another word that has this prefix. Add it to the appropriate column in the chart._

Meanings:

again   before   out of; away from   together   two   water

Prefix	Meaning	From reading	Another example
de-		de-inking process	
re-		recycling, reusing	
hydro-		sodium hydrosulfite	
di-		chlorine dioxide	
co-		collect	
pre-		precycling	

6. *What do the following **word roots** mean? Match the root with its meaning, find an example in "Paper Recycling," and then think of another word that has this root in it.*

hand   lead   make   skill   study of   wheel, circle

Root	Meaning	From reading	Another example
cycle			
duc			
ology			
tech			
manu			
fact			

7. *Find four examples of compound nouns in "Paper Recycling."*

a.  *wastepaper*

b. _____

c. _____

d. _____

Targeting

Process Terms

Scientific descriptions sometimes use the passive voice when the action itself is more important than who does the action.

1. *Look at the information about the use of the passive.*

Active Voice	subject verb object The <u>recycling company</u> <u>sorts</u> the <u>paper</u> into 30 grades.
Passive Voice	subject BE + past participle The <u>paper</u> <u>is sorted</u> into 30 grades. Note that the object in the active voice sentence above becomes subject of the passive voice sentence. No doer of the action is stated, but *the recycling company* is understood to be the doer.

2. *Here are some common phrases used in describing the paper recycling process. Write a **P** next to the ones that are in the passive.*

is/are sorted into	consists of	involves	is/are collected by
is/are made into	is/are put into	is/are processed	is/are bleached
is/are sent	send	is/are used	uses/use

3. *Complete these sentences using a passive or active phrase from the list in exercise 2. You may use the phrases more than once.*

a. The process of recycling paper _____ several steps.

b. Used paper _____ recycling bins.

c. The paper _____ different grades.

d. Recycling companies _____ the sorted paper to paper manufacturers.

e. The paper _____ into pulp.

f. Groundwood _____ newsprint.

g. A chemical process _____ on high grade white paper.

h. Manufacturers have to _____ a mechanical process to make newsprint into pulp.

i. The chemical process _____ various chemicals, such as oxygen and hydrogen peroxide.

j. High grade white paper _____ paper towels and tissues.

....

You are going to write a description of the paper recycling process or another scientific process. *Follow these steps to prepare to write. Use separate paper.*

1. Make an outline of the general steps in the process.

2. Fill in the necessary details.

3. Where would specific examples be helpful? Mark these parts of your outline with (ex).

4. Where would a transition expression help (for example, *next, after that, then*)? Mark these spots with the transition word or phrase.

As you prepare technical descriptions for your class, you will be required to show information in visual form, such as a diagram. In this assignment, you need to make a clear diagram of a basic process.

1. *Think of a basic process that you may need to explain. List the basic information you would need to include.*

2. *Consider these questions:*

What information can go in a diagram?

What information cannot go in a diagram?

What would be the clearest way to diagram the process?

Will color or other forms of highlighting help?

Will readers need an introduction or a key to help them understand the diagram?

Writing

Preparing to Write 1: Outlining Steps

Preparing to Write 2: Diagramming Basic Information

Writing About a Scientific Process

Write the description for the process of recycling paper or another scientific process. If you choose to do another scientific process, draw a diagram to show the basic process. Write an introduction and any essential information that cannot be shown in the diagram. Be sure to write an introduction to the diagram or provide a key to reading it.

WRITING TIP

Be objective. Avoid *I* and *you* in a technical description of a process.

Editing and Rewriting

Editing Checklist

Check the Content

1. *Exchange your process paper with a classmate. After you read your classmate's work, answer these questions:*

   ❏ Are all of the steps in the process complete?
   ❏ Is the tone appropriate for a scientific process?

Check the Details

2. *Read your own writing again. If necessary, revise. Add or change details. Then continue checking your paper. Use these questions:*

   ❏ Did you use process terms correctly in the passive?
   ❏ Are the verb tenses correct? Do all the subjects and verbs agree?
   ❏ Are there transition expressions to connect the steps of the process?

3. *Rewrite your process paper.*

Vocabulary Log

What words or phrases would you like to remember from this chapter? Write five to ten items in your notebook.

Grammar and Punctuation Review

Look over your writing from this chapter. What changes did you need to make in grammar and punctuation? Write them in your notebook. Review them before the next writing assignment.

Chapter 15

Is Recycling Garbage?

Recycling is a controversial issue. Some people think recycling is a waste of time and money—"a lot of garbage." Others feel the anti-recyclers are spreading false information. In this chapter you will read the pros and cons of recycling and write an argumentative essay.

Starting Point

Recycling Myths

Some statements about recycling are not true, but many people believe they are. We call these statements myths. In the debate over recycling, both sides make statements to support their opinions. Sometimes it's hard to decide what is **fact** and what is **opinion**.

With a classmate discuss these statements. Which do you think are based on fact (F)? Which are opinions (O)? Explain.

	F	O	Explanation
1. There is not a lot of landfill space left in the world.			
2. Landfills are harmful to human beings.			
3. Landfills are cheap to maintain.			
4. Recycling should be a profitable business.			
5. There are very few markets for recycled materials.			
6. Recycling saves trees.			
7. Recycling is very time-consuming for the public.			
8. Recycling has a limited potential.			
9. If the government requires manufacturers to change packaging and products, the task will be very costly for the companies.			

Not everyone thinks recycling saves resources. The writer of the following selection thinks that many beliefs about recycling are based on myths, not facts.

1. *Read the following selection written by John Tierney.*

Recycling is Garbage

[1] Back in the 1980s people suddenly became obsessed with personally handling their own garbage. Believing that there was no more room in landfills, Americans concluded that recycling was their only option. Their intentions were good and their conclusions seemed reasonable. Recycling does sometimes make sense—for some materials in some places at some times. However, the simplest and cheapest option is usually to bury garbage in an environmentally safe landfill. There is, in fact, no shortage of land; the crisis in 1987 was a false alarm. Therefore,

there's no reason to make recycling a legal or a moral imperative. Recycling may be the most wasteful activity in modern America: a waste of time and money, a waste of human and natural resources.

[2]   In the 1980s recycling was already happening voluntarily and profitably without government intervention. All this changed in 1987. Newspapers are to blame for unnecessarily alarming the public with the news of a garbage barge that was unable to find a dumpsite. The barge traveled thousands of miles, trying to unload its cargo of Long Islanders' trash, and its journey had a strange effect on people. The fears this incident produced are based on seven myths about the garbage crisis in this country.

[3]   The first myth is that we're a wicked, throwaway society. This is not true. Some say that we should be careful about the packaging our food comes in. Avoid plastic containers; go natural. In fact, plastic packaging and fast-food containers may seem wasteful, but they actually save resources and reduce trash. The typical household in Mexico City buys fewer packaged goods than an American household. However, it produces one-third more garbage, chiefly because Mexicans buy fresh foods in bulk and throw away large portions that are unused, spoiled, or stale. Lightweight plastic packaging, like plastic wrap or foam, requires much less energy to manufacture and transport than traditional alternatives like cardboard or paper. Food companies have switched to plastic packaging because they make money by using resources efficiently. A typical McDonald's discards less than two ounces of garbage for each customer served—less than what's generated by a typical meal at home. Plastic packaging is routinely criticized because it doesn't decay in landfills, but neither does most other packaging. William Rathje, an archeologist at the University of Arizona, has discovered from his excavations of landfills that paper, cardboard, and other organic materials—while technically biodegradable—tend to remain intact in the airless confines of a landfill.

[4]   The second myth is that our garbage will bury us. This, too, is not true. America today has a good deal more landfill space available than it did ten years ago. Landfills are scarce in just a few places, notably the Northeast, partly because of local economic realities, but mainly because of local politics. Environmentalists have prevented new landfills from opening because of another myth . . .

[5]   Our garbage will poison us. Again, untrue. Today's city landfills are mostly filled with innocuous materials like paper, yard waste, and construction debris. They contain small amounts of hazardous waste. So there is little reason to worry about modern landfills. Federal laws require that they be lined with clay and plastic, equipped with good drainage, covered daily with soil, and monitored for leaks.

[6]   The fourth myth is that we must achieve garbage independence. Is there a garbage crisis because New York can't handle its garbage? We don't consider it a food crisis because New York City can't grow all of its food. Garbage must be exported to landfills outside the city.

[7]   Another myth is that we're cursing future generations with our waste. A. Clark Wiseman, an economist at Gonzaga University in Spokane, WA, has calculated that if Americans keep generating garbage at current rates for 1,000 years, and if all their garbage is put in a landfill 100 yards deep, by the year 3000 this national garbage heap will fill a square piece of land 35 miles on each side. This doesn't seem like a huge problem in a country the size of the United States. Eventually, like previous landfills, the mounds of trash will be covered with grass and become a tiny addition to the nation's 150,000 square miles of park land.

[8]   The sixth myth is that we're squandering irreplaceable natural resources. Yes, a lot of trees are cut down to make one issue of a newspaper. But even more trees will probably be planted in their place. America's supply of timber has been increasing for decades. According to Jerry Taylor, the director of natural resource studies at the Cato Institute, "Paper is an agricultural product, made from trees grown specifically for paper production. Acting to conserve trees by recycling paper is like acting to conserve cornstalks by cutting back on corn consumption."

[9]   Some resources don't grow back, but when they have become scarce, such as tin and copper, we have found alternatives. Most food containers don't use any tin. Phone lines have fiber-optic cables of glass, which is made from sand—rather than copper wiring. The only resource that has been getting consistently more expensive is human time: the cost of labor has been rising for centuries. An hour of labor today buys a larger quantity of energy or raw materials than ever before. To economists, it's wasteful to expend human labor to save raw materials that are cheap today and will probably be cheaper tomorrow. Even Worldwatch Institute, an environmental group that strongly favors recycling and has often issued warnings about the earth's dwindling resources, has been persuaded that there are no foreseeable shortages of most minerals.

[10]   Finally, there is the myth that it is better to recycle than to throw away. This is the most enduring myth. By now, many experts and public officials know that the United States could simply bury its garbage, but this would divert attention from recycling programs. These programs have become a goal in and of themselves. It is more important to preserve the programs than to solve the original problem: what to do with garbage.

[11]   The usual reasons for recycling are that it saves money and protects the environment. On the surface this appears reasonable. However,

the recycling program consumes resources. It requires extra administrators and a continual public relations campaign explaining what to do with dozens of different products: recycle milk jugs but not milk cartons, index cards but not construction paper. Collecting a ton of recyclable items is three times more expensive than collecting a ton of garbage because the crews pick up less material at each stop. For each ton of glass, plastic, and metal that a truck delivers to a private recycler, the city of New York spends $200 more than it would to bury the material in a landfill. Officials hope to recover the extra cost by selling the material, but the market price of a ton has never been anywhere near $200.

[12] "We have to recognize that recycling costs money," says William Franklin, an engineer who has conducted a national study of recycling costs. At today's prices, a curbside recycling program typically adds 15 percent to the costs of waste disposal. He and other researchers conclude, though, that recycling does at least save energy. The extra fuel burned while picking up recyclables is more than offset by the energy savings from manufacturing less virgin paper, glass, and metal. "The net result of recycling is lower energy consumption and lower releases of air and water pollutants," says Richard Denison, a senior scientist at the Environmental Defense Fund.

[13] It is, however, not such a simple matter. Consider these questions: Does a 5-cent deposit on a soft drink help the environment?—Yes, but it is more expensive to collect those bottles than to do curbside recycling. Are reusable cups and plates better than disposables?—No. It actually takes more energy to manufacture the mugs and wash them. According to Martin Hocking, a chemist at the University of Victoria in British Columbia, you would have to use the mug 1,000 times before its energy-consumption-per-use is equal to the cup. Should you recycle today's newspaper?—Probably not. Recycling newsprint actually creates more water pollution than making new paper: for each ton of recycled newsprint that's produced, an extra 5,000 gallons of waste water are discharged. Should you require cloth diapers rather than plastic ones? Environmentalists have given up on this one. The cost-benefit analysis became too confusing.

[14] My advice to deal with garbage disposal is a pay-as-you-throw system. Trash is private property and people should be responsible for getting rid of it. Some cities are already charging according to how much garbage per household. When money is involved, people become more careful. They think about how they shop and they monitor their production of garbage. Once people switch to this pay-as-you-throw system, they typically throw away 10 to 15 percent less. We don't need rules, government intervention, or making people feel guilty enough to recycle.

2. **Taking marginal notes** will help you understand the article and interact with the ideas. Here are some examples of marginal note labels.

support for controlling idea	problem-solving	his 2nd point:...	example of...
definition	main idea	+ (positive aspect)	− (negative aspect)
conclusion	personal experience	topic	effect of...
two principles of...	...vs. ... (items in opposition)	cause of	no! I don't agree!

Read "Recycling is Garbage" again. Using some of the labels listed above, label the important parts in the reading. Circle key vocabulary, number the points in a list that the author is developing, and jot down your thoughts in the margin. Cross out or bracket unimportant information. Comment on what you agree or disagree with.

READING TIP

When you make marginal notes, ask yourself questions: Is this an important part? Is this just an example? Is this a fact or the author's opinion? Is this part of a list of ideas?

3. Read the following statements. Label them **F** for **fact** and **O** for **opinion**.

ANSWER KEY

   a. _____ Back in the 1980s people suddenly became obsessed with personally handling their own garbage.

   b. _____ Recycling may be the most wasteful activity in modern America: a waste of time and money, a waste of human and natural resources.

   c. _____ Plastic packaging and fast-food containers may seem wasteful, but they actually save resources and reduce trash.

   d. _____ A typical McDonald's discards less than two ounces of garbage for each customer served—less than what's generated by a typical meal at home.

e. _____ William Rathje, an archeologist at the University of Arizona, has discovered from his excavations of landfills that paper, cardboard, and other organic materials—while technically biodegradable—tend to remain intact in the airless confines of a landfill.

f. _____ Landfills are scarce in just a few places, notably the Northeast, partly because of local economic realities but mainly because of local politics.

g. _____ Federal laws require that they be lined with clay and plastic, equipped with good drainage, covered daily with soil, and monitored for leaks.

h. _____ A. Clark Wiseman, an economist at Gonzaga University in Spokane, WA, has calculated that if Americans keep generating garbage at current rates for 1,000 years, and if all their garbage is put in a landfill 100 yards deep, by the year 3000 this national garbage heap will fill a square piece of land 35 miles on each side.

i. _____ This doesn't seem like a huge problem in a country the size of the United States.

j. _____ Acting to conserve trees by recycling paper is like acting to conserve cornstalks by cutting back on corn consumption.

k. _____ It is more important to preserve the programs than to solve the original problem: what to do with garbage.

l. _____ For each ton of glass, plastic, and metal that a truck delivers to a private recycler, the city of New York spends $200 more than it would to bury the material in a landfill.

m. _____ It actually takes more energy to manufacture the mugs and wash them.

n. _____ According to Martin Hocking, a chemist at the University of Victoria in British Columbia, you would have to use the mug 1,000 times before its energy-consumption-per-use is equal to the cup.

4. _Find additional examples of fact and opinion statements in the article. Label them **F** or **O** in the margin._

5. _Participial adjectives_ (recycled, recycling) _provide information about the role of the noun they modify._

ANSWER KEY

- When the noun is the receiver or object of the action, the participial adjective usually ends in *-ed*.

  recycled *paper* = paper that has been recycled

- When the noun is the doer of the action, the participial adjective usually ends in *-ing*.

  recycling *industry* = an industry that processes used materials

Underline the appropriate form of the adjective in parentheses.

a. For each ton of *(recycling, recycled)* newsprint that's produced, an extra 5,000 gallons of waste is discharged.

b. The cost-benefit analysis became too *(confused, confusing)*.

c. The *(burned, burning)* fuel used while picking up recyclables is more than offset by the energy savings from manufacturing less virgin paper, glass, and metal.

d. Back in the 1980s, the citizens of the richest society in the history of the planet suddenly became *(obsessing, obsessed)* with personally handling their own garbage.

e. New York City depends on *(imported, importing)* food, but they don't consider that it's a food crisis.

f. Mounds of trash will eventually become *(grass-covering, grass-covered)* and will add to 150,000 square miles of park land in this country.

g. The myth that it is better to recycle than to throw away is the most *(enduring, endured)* myth.

h. By now, many experts and public officials know that America could simply bury its garbage, but this would divert attention from *(recycled, recycling)* programs.

6. *Do you agree or disagree with the writer of "Recycling is Garbage"? Is recycling necessary or typical in your country? Discuss with a partner or a small group.*

Targeting

Coherence Devices

Grammatical structures can be used to make writing coherent, that is, to give it the glue that holds ideas together and makes it easier for the reader to understand the development of ideas.

1. *Read these guidelines for making writing coherent.*

Guidelines	Examples
• parallelism Keeping items in a series parallel in structure will show the reader how much importance you put on each item. It also gives your writing power.	. . . a waste of **time** and **money**. *(nouns)* . . . a waste of **human** and **natural** resources. *(adjectives)*
• transition expressions Transition expressions can be used to make each additional idea in your argument stand out. They also emphasize the relationships between ideas.	moreover, furthermore, in addition, also *(addition)* as a result, therefore, subsequently *(cause-result)* in contrast, however, nonetheless *(contrast)* first, second, then, after that, finally, last *(process/chronology)* for/as an example, for instance *(exemplification)*
• the definite article, *the* *The* is used to show that the subsequent noun has been mentioned before and that you and your readers have a shared understanding of it.	For each ton of recyclables that a truck delivers, **the** city of New York spends $200 more than it would to bury **the** material in a landfill. Officials hope to recover **the** extra cost by selling **the** material in a landfill.
• key words or synonyms	**Acting to conserve** trees by recycling paper is like **acting to conserve** cornstalks by cutting back on corn consumption. *(repeating key words)*

Guidelines	Examples
	For each ton of **recyclables** that a truck delivers, the city of New York spends $200 more than it would to bury **the material** in a landfill. *(synonyms)*
If it's hard to find good synonyms or your writing sounds too repetitious, use substitute parts of speech, such as pronouns, adverbs, verbs, adjectives, or phrases.	*he, she, it, they, one, them, their, who, which, that* (pronouns)
	then, there, that way, thus, so (adverbs)
	do, does, did (verbs)
	this, that, these, those, such, mine, yours, many, some (adjectives)
	the former, the latter (phrases)

Place key words closer together in a paragraph by shifting between the active and the passive voice.	It's not enough just to recycle. You are not really recycling if you don't purchase goods made from **recycled materials. Recyclable materials** <u>must be processed</u> into
	            passive
	new products. These products <u>must be purchased, used, and recycled</u>.
	        passive
	This is called closing the loop.

2. *Complete the following paragraph, using coherence devices. In some cases, you may need to make incomplete words parallel. Refer to the article "Recycling is Garbage," pages 189–192, if you need some help.*

ANSWER KEY

The first myth is that we're a wicked throwaway society.

_____*This*_____ is not true. Some people say that we should
      (a)

be careful about the packaging our food comes in. Avoid plastic con-

tainers; go natural. Plastic packaging and fast-food containers may

seem wasteful, but _____ actually save resources
           (b)

and reduce trash. The typical household in Mexico City buys fewer

packaged goods than an American _____.
  (c)

_____, it produces one-third more garbage, chiefly
  (d)

because Mexicans buy fresh foods in bulk and throw away large

portions _____ are unused, spoiled, or stale.
  (e)

Lightweight plastic packaging—such as plastic wrap or foam—

requires much less energy to manufact_____ and
  (f)

transport_____ than traditional alternatives like
  (g)

cardboard or paper. Food companies have switched to plastic

packaging because _____ is more energy efficient,
  (h)

_____ making money. A typical McDonald's discards
  (i)

less than two ounces of garbage for each customer served—less than

what's generated by a typical meal at home. Plastic packaging is

routinely criticized because _____ doesn't decay
  (j)

in landfills, but neither _____ most other packaging.
  (k)

William Rathje, an archeologist at the University of Arizona, has

discovered from his excavations of landfills that paper, cardboard,

and other organic materials, _____ technically
  (l)

biodegradable, tend to remain intact.

Writing

Preparing to Write: Discussing the Issues

You are going to write a paper arguing for or against the issues in "Recycling is Garbage" on pages 189–192. Follow these steps to prepare your argument.

1. *Discuss with classmates the following facts and opinions of the pro-recyclers.*

According to the American Forest & Paper Association, use of recovered paper by US paper mills grew from 11.7% in 1975 to 33.4% in 1997.

• • •

Curbside recycling programs are relatively new. They can be more cost effective by changing truck designs and collection schedules and by increasing the amount of material collected.

• • •

Demand for wood is rising and the cost of wood has gone up.

• • •

Incinerators are also more expensive to build and operate than recycling programs.

• • •

Recycling increases industrial competitiveness, reduces manufacturing costs, and creates jobs.

• • •

Recycling reduces natural resource damage and pollution that arise when extracting raw materials and manufacturing new products.

• • •

Numerous cities have calculated that their per-ton recycling costs are lower than per-ton garbage collection and disposal costs.

• • •

Percentage of materials left in our garbage after recycling:

newsprint	54%
magazines	70%
office paper	57%
corrugated boxes	45%
glass containers	74%
steel cans	47%
aluminum cans	34%
plastic soda bottles	59%
total	54%

• • •

If a typical household had to pay for the cost of recycling, the cost would be $2 per month.

• • •

Landfills can be major sources of water and air pollution since the liquid that drains from beneath a landfill contains a number of toxic pollutants.

• • •

Recycling is not just an alternative to traditional solid waste disposal. It is the foundation for large manufacturing industries in the US that use recyclable materials.

• • •

The United States is saving enough energy through recycling to provide electricity for 9 million homes.

• • •

2. *Decide which information in the newspaper clippings and in the selection you will use in your argument.*

Things I agree with:

Things I don't agree with:

3. *As you studied in previous chapters, writers use certain verbs and expressions to report information from a source. To practice these typical summary expressions and vocabulary (in bold below), complete these sentences with information from "Recycling is Garbage" or from Preparing to Write, exercise 1.*

a. **In** John Tierney's **article** "_____,"

   he discusses the myths of recycling. **According to**

   _____, recycling is garbage.

b. **The author argues that** _____

   _____

c. **The author further states that** _____

   _____

d. **Furthermore, the author maintains that** _____

   _____

Write an essay in which you agree with or attack the points in "Recycling is Garbage." Be sure to include an introduction and a conclusion. You may want to refer to Chapter 11, pages 135–139, for suggestions about organizing an argumentative paper.

Writing an Argumentative Paper

Editing and Rewriting

Editing for Problems with Coherence

....

Good argument writing has a controlling idea, logical organization, and coherence. The argument flows smoothly from point to point, and the writer uses devices to hold his or her ideas together.

Revise the following paragraphs by making them more coherent. If necessary, refer to Targeting: Coherence Devices, pages 195–197, for a review of ways to make writing coherent. Rewrite the paragraphs on separate paper.

a. In the 1980s recycling was already happening voluntarily and profit without government intervention. All of voluntary recycling happening without government intervention changed in 1978. Newspapers are to blame for unnecessarily alarming the public with the news of a garbage barge. The garbage barge was unable to find a dumpsite. The barge traveled thousands of miles, trying to unload the barge's cargo of Long Islanders' trash. The journey of the barge had a strange effect on America. The garbage barge incident produced fears. The fears are based on seven myths about the garbage crisis in the U.S.

b. Consider these questions: Does a 5-cent deposit on a soft drink help the environment? Yes, a 5-cent deposit helps the environment, but a 5-cent deposit on a soft drink is more expensive to collect than curbside recycling is to do. Are reusable cups and plates better than disposables? No, reusable cups and plates are not better than disposables. It actually takes more energy to manufacture ceramic mugs and washing the mugs. According to Martin Hocking, you would have to use a mug 1,000 times before the mug's energy-consumption-per-use is equal to the cup. Martin Hocking is a chemist at the University of Victoria in British Columbia. Should you recycle today's newspaper? You probably shouldn't recycle today's newspaper. Recycling newsprint actually creates more water pollution than make new paper: for each ton of recycled newsprint that's produced, an extra 5,000 gallons of waste water are discharged. Requiring cloth diapers rather than plastic diapers? Environmentalists have given up on whether you should require cloth diapers rather than plastic diapers. The cost-benefit analysis of requiring cloth diapers became too confusing.

Editing Checklist

Check the Content

1. *Exchange your argumentative paper with a classmate. After you read your classmate's work, answer these questions:*

   ❑ Is there a strong statement of the point of view?
   ❑ Is this point of view supported with details or examples?
   ❑ Is there an introduction and conclusion?

Check the Details

2. *Read your own writing again. If necessary, revise. Add or change details. Then continue checking your paper. Use these questions:*

   ❑ Is the passive voice used correctly and effectively for coherence?
   ❑ Did you use coherence devices?
   ❑ Are there transition expressions to connect your main points?
   ❑ Did you include sentence variety?

3. *Rewrite your argumentative paper.*

Vocabulary Log

What words or phrases would you like to remember from this chapter? Write five to ten items in your notebook.

Grammar and Punctuation Review

Look over your writing from this chapter. What changes did you need to make in grammar and punctuation? Write them in your notebook.

Class Activity   A Local Recycling Project

The University of Wisconsin-Madison sold reusable plastic mugs to its students. The mugs cost $2, but the university gave the students a 20% discount on drinks. In addition, the mugs were 14-ounce rather than the typical 12-ounce size. Before they sold the mugs, the school was buying 400,000 Styrofoam™ cups a year, which were used once and then thrown in the garbage. Even little changes in behavior can have a big effect on a garbage problem. What changes could be made at your school?

1 Choose a waste problem at your campus.

2 Decide on a way to precycle or recycle in order to reduce the amount of waste.

3 Create a poster or write a letter to the school newspaper to advertise the need for recycling and to show the plan for dealing with the problem.

Reference

BUSINESS LETTER FORMAT

The format of a business letter is more formal than a personal letter.

This example is the **full block style**. All the lines of text are lined up on the left.

First and last name Street address City, Country	Carl Brodschi 414 River Road Louisville, KY 40207
Date	March 20, 1998
Name and address of person you are writing to	Suzanne Grant Director, Housing Office Boston University 66 Bay State Road Boston, MA 02215
Salutation	Dear Ms. Grant:
Text of the letter	I will be attending Boston University next year. Please send me information about student housing and an application form.
Closing statement	Thank you very much.
Closing phrase	Sincerely,
Signature	*Carl Brodschi*
Printed name	Carl Brodschi

This is the **modified block style**. The first line of each paragraph may be indented five spaces. The address of the sender, the closing phrase, and the signature are all on the right.

Sender's name and address	Carl Brodschi 414 River Road Louisville, KY 40207
Date	March 20, 1998
Name and address of person you are writing to	Suzanne Grant Director, Housing Office Boston University 66 Bay State Road Boston, MA 02215
Salutation	Dear Ms. Grant:
Text of the letter	I will be attending Boston University next year. Please send me information about student housing and an application form.
Closing statement	Thank you very much.
Closing phrase	Sincerely,
Signature	*Carl Brodschi*
Printed name	Carl Brodschi

INFINITIVES AND GERUNDS AS OBJECTS OF VERBS

Rules	Examples
1. Some verbs can only take an infinitive (*to* + verb) object.	I **agreed to do** the work.
2. Some verbs can only take a gerund (verb + *ing*) object.	I don't **mind doing** this kind of work.
3. Some verbs can take either an infinitive or a gerund object.	I **like doing** this kind of work. I **like to do** this kind of project.
4. Some verbs take an infinitive if there is a noun phrase or pronoun object before the infinitive.	He **told me to do** it. She **told the students to do** it.
5. A small number of verbs take an object and a "*to*-less" infinitive.	They **made me do** it. She **let the students do** it.

	infinitive	gerund	either	noun phrase/ pronoun object before infinitive	"*to*-less" infinitive		infinitive	gerund	either	noun phrase/ pronoun object before infinitive	"*to*-less" infinitive
admit		✔				believe				✔	
advise		✔		✔		bother	✔				
(can/can't) afford	✔					care	✔				
agree	✔					cause			✔	✔	
aim	✔					choose	✔			✔	
allow		✔		✔		claim	✔				
appear	✔					coerce	✔			✔	
appoint				✔		come	✔				
appreciate		✔				complete		✔			
arrange	✔					consent to		✔			
ask	✔			✔		consider		✔		✔	
attempt			✔			continue			✔		
avoid		✔				control		✔			
be	✔					convince				✔	
(can't) bear			✔			dare	✔			✔	
beg	✔			✔		decide	✔				
begin			✔			declare				✔	
						decline	✔				

	infinitive	gerund	either	noun phrase/pronoun object before infinitive	"to-less" infinitive			infinitive	gerund	either	noun phrase/pronoun object before infinitive	"to-less" infinitive
decrease		✔					help				✔	✔
defer		✔					hesitate	✔				
defy		✔		✔			hire				✔	
delay		✔					hope	✔				
demand	✔						imagine		✔		✔	
deny		✔					implore				✔	
describe		✔					incite		✔		✔	
deserve			✔				increase			✔		
desire	✔						induce				✔	
despise		✔					instruct				✔	
determine	✔						intend	✔			✔	
detest		✔					investigate		✔			
direct				✔			invite				✔	
discover	✔						judge	✔				
dislike		✔					keep		✔			
dread		✔					know				✔	
drive				✔			lead				✔	
educate				✔			learn	✔				
empower				✔			let					✔
enable				✔			like		✔			
encourage				✔			long	✔				
endeavor	✔						love		✔			
endure		✔					make					✔
enjoy		✔					manage	✔				
entitle				✔			mean		✔		✔	
escape		✔					mind		✔			
excuse		✔					miss		✔			
expect	✔			✔			motivate	✔			✔	
fail	✔						need			✔	✔	
favor		✔					neglect			✔		
fear		✔					notify				✔	
find				✔			object to		✔			
finish		✔					oblige	✔				
forbid				✔			offer	✔				
forget			✔				omit		✔			
get		✔					order				✔	
give up		✔					permit		✔		✔	
go		✔					persuade				✔	
guess				✔			plan	✔				
happen	✔						pledge	✔				
hate			✔				postpone		✔			

	infinitive	gerund	either	noun phrase/ pronoun object before infinitive	"to-less" infinitive
prefer			✔	✔	
prepare	✔			✔	
pretend	✔				
proceed	✔				
promise	✔			✔	
propose		✔			
prove	✔				
put off		✔			
quit			✔		
recall		✔			
refuse	✔				
regret		✔			
remember			✔	✔	
remind				✔	
report				✔	
request				✔	
require		✔		✔	
resent		✔			
resist		✔			
resolve	✔				
resume		✔			
return	✔			✔	
risk		✔			
rule	✔				
save		✔			
say	✔				
see		✔			✔
seek	✔				
seem	✔				

	infinitive	gerund	either	noun phrase/ pronoun object before infinitive	"to-less" infinitive
select				✔	
send				✔	
(can/can't) stand		✔			
start			✔		
state				✔	
stimulate				✔	
stop			✔		
strive	✔				
struggle	✔				
suggest		✔			
suppose	✔				
swear	✔				
teach				✔	
tell				✔	
tempt				✔	
tend	✔				
think				✔	
threaten	✔				
train				✔	
trust				✔	
try			✔		
understand			✔		
undertake	✔				
urge				✔	
wait	✔				
want				✔	
warn				✔	
wish	✔			✔	

IRREGULAR SIMPLE PAST TENSE VERBS

Base	Simple Past	Past Participle	Base	Simple Past	Past Participle
awake	awoke	awoken	leave	left	left
bear	born	born	lend	lent	lent
beat	beat	beaten	let	let	let
become	became	become	lie	lay	lain
begin	began	begun	light	lit/lighted	lit/lighted
bend	bent	bent	lost	lost	lost
bet	bet	bet	make	made	made
bid	bid	bid	mean	meant	meant
bite	bit	bitten	meet	met	met
bleed	bled	bled	prove	proved	proven
blow	blew	blown	put	put	put
break	broke	broken	quit	quit	quit
bring	brought	brought	read	read	read
build	built	built	rid	rid	rid
burn	burnt/burned	burnt/burned	ride	rode	ridden
burst	burst	burst	ring	rang	rung
buy	bought	bought	rise	rose	risen
cast	cast	cast	run	ran	run
catch	caught	caught	say	said	said
choose	chose	chosen	see	saw	seen
come	came	come	seek	sought	sought
cost	cost	cost	sell	sold	sold
creep	crept	crept	send	sent	sent
cut	cut	cut	set	set	set
deal	dealt	dealt	shake	shook	shaken
dig	dug	dug	shine	shone	shone
dive	dove	dived	shoot	shot	shot
	(British: dived)		shrink	shrank	shrunk
do	did	done	shut	shut	shut
draw	drew	drawn	sing	sang	sung
dream	dreamt/dreamed	dreamt/dreamed	sink	sank	sunk
drink	drank	drunk	sit	sat	sat
drive	drove	driven	sleep	slept	slept
eat	ate	eaten	slide	slid	slid
fall	fell	fallen	slit	slit	slit
feed	fed	fed	speak	spoke	spoken
feel	felt	felt	spend	spent	spent
fight	fought	fought	spin	spun	spun
find	found	found	split	split	split
fit	fit	fit	spread	spread	spread
fly	flew	flown	spring	sprang	sprung
forbid	forbid/forbade	forbidden	stand	stood	stood
forget	forgot	forgotten	steal	stole	stolen
forgive	forgave	forgiven	stick	stuck	stuck
freeze	froze	frozen	sting	stung	stung
get	got	gotten	strike	struck	struck
		(British: got)	swear	swore	sworn
give	gave	given	sweep	swept	swept
go	went	gone	swim	swam	swum
grind	ground	ground	swing	swung	swung
grow	grew	grown	take	took	taken
hang	hung	hung	teach	taught	taught
have	had	had	tear	tore	torn
hear	heard	heard	tell	told	told
hide	hid	hidden/hid	think	thought	thought
hit	hit	hit	throw	threw	thrown
hold	held	held	wake	woke	woken
hurt	hurt	hurt	wear	wore	worn
keep	kept	kept	wet	wet	wet
knit	knit	knitted	win	won	won
know	knew	known	wind	wound	wound
lay	laid	laid	withdraw	withdrew	withdrawn
lead	led	led			

NONCOUNT NOUNS

Some nouns do not have a plural form because we cannot count them. We call these *noncount* nouns. Follow these rules when you use a noncount noun.

Rules	Examples
Noncount nouns are singular. If they are the subject of the sentence, the verb must be singular, too.	The **milk is** on the table. His **news is** not good. The **homework was** easy.
Do not use **a** or **an** with a noncount noun.	We need **milk**.
Use a quantity expression to make a noncount noun countable.	Please get **a gallon of milk**. I have **lots of homework** tonight.

Here are some common noncount nouns.

Category	Example
Groups of similar items	art, clothing, equipment, food, fruit, furniture, garbage, grammar, homework, information, luggage, mail, money, music, news, research, slang, traffic, vocabulary, work
Liquids	beer, blood, coffee, cream, gasoline, honey, juice, milk, oil, shampoo, soda, soup, tea, water, wine
Things that can be cut into smaller pieces	bread, butter, cheese, cotton, film, glass, gold, ice, iron, meat, paper, silver, wood
Things that have very small parts	dirt, flour, grass, hair, rice, sand, sugar
Gases	air, fog, pollution, smog, smoke, steam
Ideas that you cannot touch	advice, anger, beauty, communication, education, fun, happiness, health, help, love, luck, peace, sleep, space, time, truth, wealth
Fields of study	business administration, engineering, nursing
Activities	soccer, swimming, tennis, traveling
Diseases and illnesses	cancer, cholera, flu, heart disease, malaria, polio, small-pox, strep throat
Facts or events of nature	darkness, electricity, fire, fog, heat, light, lightning, rain, snow, sunshine, thunder, weather, wind
Languages	Arabic, Chinese, Turkish, Russian

TRANSITION EXPRESSIONS

When you combine sentences or ideas, transition expressions help make your ideas clear.

Rules	Examples
Start with two separate ideas or sentences.	I ate breakfast. I went to the store at 10:00 A.M.
Combine the ideas with a **preposition**.	I went to the store **after** breakfast.
Combine the ideas with a **subordinate conjunction**.	I went to the store **after** I ate breakfast. I ate breakfast **before** I went to the store.
Combine the ideas with **an adverbial expression**.	I ate breakfast. **After that,** I went to the store. I went to the store. **Before that,** I ate breakfast.

Here are some common transition expressions.

Transition Expressions	Examples
Time in a Sequence **Prepositions:** after, before, until, since, prior to **Subordinate Conjunctions:** after, before, until (till), once, ever since **Adverbial Expressions:** *to express time before the present:* before that, beforehand, formerly, in the past, earlier, (not) long ago, at first *to express time now:* at present, presently, at this point/time, nowadays, currently *to express time after:* after that, afterward, later, later on, soon after *to express time in the future:* in the future	We waited **until** 3:15. We waited **until** they came. We weren't angry **at first.** **At first**, we weren't angry.
Listing **Adverbial Expressions:** first, in the first place, in the second place, later on, then, subsequently, from then on, following that, after that, next, finally, last *including length of time:* before long, immediately, from then on, following that, since then	**First**, try to write down the problem. **Then**, telephone the landlord.

Transition Expressions	Examples
Time: Simultaneous	
Preposition: during	They watch TV **during** dinner.
Subordinate Conjunctions: when, as, while, as long as, whenever	They watch TV **when** they eat dinner.
Adverbial Expressions: meanwhile, in the meantime, at the same time, at that time	I waited in line at the ticket counter. **Meanwhile**, my father returned the rental car.
Contrast	
Prepositions: unlike, in contrast to	**Unlike** my sister, I like cold weather.
Subordinate Conjunctions: but, while, whereas	I like cold weather, **but** my sister doesn't.
Adverbial Expressions: however, in contrast, on the other hand, by/in comparison, in fact, on the contrary	I like cold weather. My sister, **on the other hand**, hates it.
Contrast: Concession	
Prepositions: despite, in spite of, regardless of	They had the party outside **despite** the weather.
Subordinate Conjunctions: although, though, even though, while, in spite of/regardless of/despite the fact that	They had the party outside **although** it looked like rain.
Adverbial Expressions: even so, just the same, after all, anyhow, anyway, admittedly, regardless	It looked like rain. **Even so**, they had the party outside.
Contrast: Dismissal and Replacement	
Prepositions: instead of, rather than	They ate a snack **instead of** a big dinner.
Adverbial Expressions: either way, in any case/event, at any rate, no matter how/what, instead	**No matter what** they decide, *I* am going to go on that trip.
Cause-Effect, Results, Reasons	
Prepositions: because of, as a result of, due to, owing to, on account of, in view of, since	She was unhappy **because of** her living situation.
Subordinate Conjunctions: because, since, as, now that, in view of/on account of/because of/due to the fact that	She was unhappy **because** she didn't like her roommates.
	Since her roommates never talked to her, she didn't feel comfortable in her apartment.
Adverbial Expressions: for this reason, because of this, as a result, therefore, so	Her roommates almost never spoke. **Because of this**, she was very unhappy in her apartment.

Transition Expressions	Examples
Condition	
Subordinate Conjunctions: if, unless, whether (or not), even if, only if, in case that, provided that, on condition that, supposing that	**If** it rains, we won't go to the beach. We'll go to the beach **unless** it rains.
Consequence	
Adverbial Expressions: in that case, if so, then, otherwise, or else, if not, under those circumstances	If you want to come with us, that's fine. **Otherwise**, we'll meet you there.
Examples	
Preposition: such as	I like sports **such as** ice-skating that keep you warm in the winter.
Adverbial Expressions: for example, as an example, for instance, e.g.	Some winter sports are better than others. **For example**, ice-skating keeps you warm and is great exercise.
Conclusion	
Adverbial Expressions: in conclusion, in summary, to summarize, all in all	**All in all**, we had a wonderful time.
Addition	
Preposition: in addition to	On their trip they visited Alaska **in addition to** the Canadian Rockies.
Adverbial Expressions: also, in addition, moreover, likewise, similarly	He didn't want to spend so much time away. **In addition**, it was too expensive.

Answer Key

I On the Job

CHAPTER 1

Starting Point *(pages 2–3)*

1. d; 2. h; 3. i; 4. a; 5. j; 6. e; 7. f; 8. b; 9. c; 10. g

Reading *(pages 3–5)*

2. *(page 4)*
a. 9; b. 5; c. 1; d. 7; e. 6; f. 12; g. 10; h. 2; i. 11; j. 4; k. 3; l. 8; m. 13
3. *(page 4)*
a. respect; b. mass; c. big deal; d. goals; e. persistent; f. treat
4. *(page 5)*
b, f, j

Targeting: Collocations Related to Work *(pages 5–7)*

2. *(page 7)*
b. as; c. do; d. created, set up; e. with; f. create/design/set up;
g. manage/direct/run/administer; h. do

CHAPTER 2

Reading 1 *(pages 10–11)*

3. *(page 11)*
Katerina Long: in charge of, Promoted to . . . handling, Managed;
Maria Fernandez: Managed, Supervised, Responsible for, In charge of,
Responsible for

Reading 2 *(pages 12–14)*

2. *(page 13)*
tenure: whether you *stay with one company for life or move from company to company*
recruitment: whether companies *hire from within or bring new people in with experience in other companies*
personal connections: whether *people are hired and promoted because of their personal connections*
women in the workforce: whether women *are considered permanent or temporary workers*
4. *(page 14)*

recruitment	noun	recruit (V, N) recruiter (N)
promotion	noun	promote (V)
specialization	noun	specialize (V) specialty (N)
loyalty	noun	loyal (adj)
supervisor	noun	supervise (V) supervising, supervised (adj)
performance	noun	perform (V) performer (N) performing (adj)
virtually	adv	virtual (adj)
assured	verb	assurance (N) assuring, assured (adj)
economy	noun	economize (V) economic (adj) economically (adv)

5. *(page 14)*
adjective endings: -ing, -ed, -ious, -ual, -ic
noun endings: -ment, -(a)tion, -y, -or, -er, -ance, -ige
verb endings: -y, -e, -ize, -ise
adverb endings: -ly

Targeting: Ways to Connect Ideas *(pages 15–17)*

2. *(pages 16–17)*
a. Some; b. For example; c. After working; d. However; e. each move/company, these moves; f. on the other hand; g. this degree; h. this;
i. These examples; j. One; k. Another, The other; l. Another; m. these/such;
n. for instance/for example; o. Similarly/Also; p. however; q. these

Preparing to Write 1: Analyzing the Style and Format of Formal Letters *(pages 18–19)*

1. *(page 18)*
g, i, b, c, a, j, e, h, d, f

Editing for Verb Tense Errors *(pages 20–23)*

2. *(pages 22–23)*
a. am looking, will be able to/can contribute
b. majored, am looking, were
c. would like, ~~have~~ had, ~~have~~ offered
d. requires, ~~will~~ graduate, will call, look/am looking
e. was responsible, ~~were~~ included, appreciate/would appreciate

CHAPTER 3

Reading 1 *(pages 25–27)*

1. *(page 25)*
Employment, Public Services, Public Accommodations, Telecommunications, Miscellaneous
2. *(page 26)*
a. prohibits; b. reasonable, disabilities; c. available, accessible; d. deny;
e. modify, restructure; f. protects, disabled; g. right
4. *(page 27)*
1. adjective; 2. noun; 3. noun; 4. noun; 5. adjective; 6. adjective; 7. adjective; 8. verb; 9. verb; 10. noun; 11. adjective

Reading 2 *(pages 28–32)*

2. *(page 29)*
one topic with facts and examples
4. *(page 31)*
a. illegal   A person with a disability might not "pass" a medical exam but this wouldn't mean that he or she was unable to do the job.
b. legal   This is a legitimate requirement for a pilot of an airplane.
c. legal   Being able to hear is a legitimate job requirement in a child care center.
d. illegal   Someone with a disability may not be able to drive.
e. illegal   This would limit access for someone who is blind in a facility open to the public.
f. illegal   This limits access for people with disabilities.
g. legal   This is a private house, not a building open to the public, so an elevator is not required.
h. illegal   Changing the desk is a reasonable accommodation that the company must make.
i. legal   Although this might be contested by a very capable individual in a wheelchair, it is likely that being in a wheelchair would make it difficult to teach physical education effectively.
j. legal   This accommodates the disabled person's needs.
5. *(page 31)*
b. 2; c. 1; d.2; e. 1; f. 3; g. 2; h. 1 or 2; i. 3
6. *(pages 31–32)*
b. S, G; c. G, S; d. G, S; e. S, G

Editing and Rewriting: Editing for Consistency in Charts and Lists *(pages 33–35)*

2. *(pages 34–35)*
a. improve employee relations; b. check; c. old (lowercase);
d. make some changes; e. Study the products

2 The Living Language

CHAPTER 4

Reading (pages 39–45)

2. (page 40)
a. 1. [3, 4]; 2. [2]; 3. [1] 4. [5]; b. 3; c. 2, 3; d. the following strategies, such as, First, Also, After finding, For example
3. (page 41)
a. ream; b. resolve; c. conflicts; d. premise; e. adversarial; f. cooperates; g. strategies; h. clarify; i. objectives; j. objective; k. judgmental; l. criticize; m. perspective; n. concession
4. (pages 41–42)

negotiate	verb	negotiation (N) negotiator (N)
adversarial	adjective	adversary (N)
resolution	noun	resolve (V)
effective	adjective	effectively (adv) effect (N)
clarify	verb	clarity (N)
statements	noun	state (V) stated (adj)
acknowledge	verb	acknowledgment (N)
concessions	noun	concede (V)
collaboratively	adverb	collaborative (adj) collaboration (N) collaborator (N)

5. (page 42)
make small concessions; be indirect about demands; don't criticize/be nonjudgmental; be unemotional/do not use loaded words; express your own perspective; sandwich negative ideas into positive statements; get information in the open; share common goals/cooperate/show a willingness to work collaboratively; listen actively; clarify and restate.
6. (pages 42–43)
too direct about demands, does not show a willingness to work together, does not concede; it's critical and judgmental (has loaded words); uses an inappropriate tone for a formal letter
7. (pages 44–45)
Possible answers
a. I am writing to you because I am very disappointed with the athletic program. (Techniques: remove loaded language and focus on my perspective)
b. The facilities and the instructors for the courses are not at the level which I am accustomed to. (Techniques: remove loaded language and focus on my perspective)
c. Delete this one completely. (sarcastic and noncollaborative)
d. I'm sure you can understand that, with the tuition we pay, we would expect to have better sports facilities and programs. (Technique: establish a collaborative approach)
e. Would it be possible to work out a plan to acquire new equipment, have professionals do training clinics for the instructors, and offer more of a variety of courses? (Techniques: be less direct about demands and show a willingness to work collaboratively)
f. Also, if the building were open later in the evening, more students could take advantage of the facilities. (Techniques: be less direct about demand and unemotional) "Sandwiching" would be "It's great that the building is open at night. However, could the hours be extended?" (Good news, bad news, and then, if possible, good news again. Sometimes it's an open-face sandwich.)
g. I would appreciate having the opportunity to talk with you about possible ideas. I will telephone to find out a time that would be convenient. (Technique: avoid critical language and show a willingness to work collaboratively)

CHAPTER 5

Reading 1 (pages 47–48)

2. (page 47)
Her husband wants her to learn Russian, but she has no time. Her husband and his friends speak Russian at home and she feels left out.
5. (page 48)
a. compromise; b. overcome; c. priority; d. left; e. point; f. crash; g. insist; h. overcome

Reading 2 (pages 49–52)

1. (page 49)
Two employees speak their native language and it bothers English-speaking employees.
4. (page 50)
a. handle; b. insist on; c. implementing; d. restrictions; e. discriminatory; f. hostile; g. sued; h. claimed; i. swearing; j. prohibited; k. privilege; l. friction; m. legitimate; n. broad-reaching; o. unduly; p. potential; q. ultimately
5. (pages 50–51)
a. implementing language restrictions; b. people feel left out or uncomfortable; c. 1
6. (page 51)
a. Note: The author of the FAQ says, "a situation where . . . " This is common in everyday speech. However, "a situation in which" is correct.
b. two employees
c. speaking to each other in another language
d. implementing language restrictions in the workplace
e. the rule
f. non-Spanish-speaking coworkers
g. the four Hispanic employees
h. an employee's
i. the store Note: The author of the FAQ uses "they" to refer to the store; earlier in the sentence, he means (but does not say) "the owners of the store."
j. the rule
7. (page 52)
Answers will vary. Some possibilities:
a. two employees keep talking to one another in their native language; this makes the people they work with unhappy
b. speaking Spanish was necessary to complete bank business or when the employees were helping Spanish-speaking customers
c. workers were unhappy and uncomfortable when Spanish was spoken
d. not; employees don't have a right to speak their language at work
e. enforce an English-only restriction; employees had to interact with a customer

Targeting: Ways to Express Demands (pages 52–54)

2. (pages 53–54)
Answers will vary. Some possibilities:
a. to speak English only; b. speaking; c. the employee to speak Spanish; d. prohibited; e. them to speak English only; f. to require English; g. they speak English; h. required to, that, speak; i. should (not) be; j. it was; require

Editing and Rewriting: Editing for Errors in Article Use (pages 56–58)

2. (page 58)
a. the; b. —; c. a; d. the; e. the; f. a; g. a; h. —; i. The; j. the; k. —; l. —; m. a; n. the; o. —; p. the

CHAPTER 6

Reading 1 (pages 60–65)

2. (page 63)
a. other children; b. copy; c. with different levels of power and control; d. complicated; e. talk about with pride; f. feeling of closeness; g. the way they relate; h. solution where each gives up something; i. made it less serious; j. give up

3. *(pages 64–65)*
a. MI; b. SD; c. SD; d. MI; e. MI; f. SD; g. MI; h. SD
4. *(page 65)*
Girls: expected not to boast or show that they think they are better; do not give orders; express preferences as suggestions; are not as bossy, don't want center stage, and don't challenge each other directly; compromise; are indirect; are openly cooperative; are egalitarian except in pretend parent-child relationships
Boys: give orders and make them stick; tell stories and jokes; sidetrack or challenge the stories and jokes of others; argue about rules of games; appeal to rules, boast of their skill, and argue who is best; insist; threaten violence; are openly competitive; are hierarchical

Reflect on Reading *(page 65)*

a and d

Reading 2 *(pages 66–68)*

2. *(page 66)* a
3. *(page 67)* a
4. *(page 67)* b
5. *(page 68)* a
7. *(page 68)* a. empowered; b. criticism; c. business; d. clear;
e. egalitarian; f. stereotype; g. ambassador; h. question; i. isolation;
j. mainstream

Targeting Collocations: Verbs to Report Point of View *(pages 68–70)*

2. *(page 70)*
a. 5; b. 3; c. 1, 4; d. 5, 6; e. 1, 2, 4; f. 1, 2, 4

Editing and Rewriting: Editing for Sentence Completeness *(pages 72–73)*

2. *(page 73)*
a. is very different; b. "male, for example" or "For example, they speak . . ."; c. *(correct)*; d. shocked because; e. differently is debatable;
f. *(correct)*; g. ideas. They; h. style. They; i. women are different;
j. styles because

3 Personality Plus
CHAPTER 7
Reading *(pages 78–82)*

3. *(page 80)*
a. view of the future; b. evidence, are born with; c. brain chemicals;
d. positive feelings about oneself; e. in control; f. starts to work;
g. true reasons
4. *(pages 80–81)*
a. S; b. D; c. D; d. D; e. D; f. D; g. D; h. S; i. S; j. S; k. S; l. D
5. *(page 81)*
a. twins; b. of the twins; c. a man raised in an uneducated fishing family; d. his twin; e. the twin girls; f. twin; g. genes; h. serotonin and dopamine; i. serotonin and dopamine; j. Lykken and Tellegen
6. *(page 82)*
a, c, g, h, i

Targeting: Prefixes and Roots *(pages 82–84)*

a. with, together; b. mind; c. alike; d. bottom; e. feeling; f. skill; g. many, great; h. one, all; i. bad, ill; j. place, put

Preparing to Write 1: Understanding Essay Exam Questions *(pages 84–85)*

1. *(pages 84–85)*
b. D; c. CC; d. EX; e. C-R; f. CL or D; g. C-R; h. P; i. CC; j. EX; k. P; l.CL

Preparing to Write 2: Organizing Essay Exam Responses *(pages 85–86)*

1. *(pages 85–86)*
Answers will vary. Possible answers:
b.   There are four traits of happy people.

c.   A biologically based temperament is a personality that is predetermined by genetic make-up.
d.   There are several studies that link genes to emotions.
e.   Critics of the research on the genetic link to happiness find fault with several aspects of the research.
f.   There are stronger arguments for genetic influence on a person's happiness than against.

Editing and Rewriting: Editing for Punctuation *(pages 86–89)*

2. *(page 89)*
a, b, d, i, m

CHAPTER 8
Starting Point *(pages 92–93)*

1. *(pages 92–93)*
a. It's written in the stars.; b. Opposites attract.; c. Every product-oriented person needs a process-oriented colleague.; d. Great minds think alike.; e. Blood will tell.

Reading *(pages 93–99)*

2. *(pages 94–95)*
A.
a. blood—cheerfulness; b. black bile—sadness; c. phlegm—a lack of energy; d. yellow bile—anxiety and irritability
B.
1.   examples: tests to determine personality types
2.   astrologers
3.

	Positive	Negative
Type O	strong leaders who inspire others; goal-oriented	status-seeking and greedy
Type A	perfectionist; orderly and attentive	perfectionist; picky, inflexible
Type B	independent, flexible, passionate, creative	unpredictable, impatient
Type AB	organized, honest	unforgiving, nit-picking, conservative

C. Positive: work quickly
Negative: consider fewer ideas; less creative
group convinces itself that it is right even when all signs indicate the opposite (group think)
D. counseling—how to communicate effectively
most important—being a good listener
new research—one person gave in to the other's demands in the most successful relationships
3. *(page 96)*
a. O; b. O; c. O; d. R; e. O; f. R
4. *(page 96)*

categorize	V	*categorization, category (N)*
energy	N	*energize (V); energetic (adj.)*
irritability	N	*irritable (adj); irritate (V); irritation (N)*
biological	adj	*biology (N); biologically (adv)*
perfectionist	N	*perfect (adj, V); perfection (N); perfectly (adv)*
compatibility	N	*compatible (adj)*
inspire	V	*inspiration (N); inspiring, inspired (adj)*
optimism	N	*optimist (N—person); optimistic (adj); optimistically (adv)*
astrologer	N	*astrologist (N—person); astrology (N)*

5. *(page 97)*
adj: -al, -ible, -able, -ic, -ing, -ed; *verb:* -ize, -e; *adv:* -ly; N (person): -ist, -er; N (not person): -ion, -y, -ity, -(a)tion
6. *(pages 97–98)*

a.	quality or condition of	condition of being nervous	variety
b.	living	dealing with life pro-cesses or living things	biography
c.	quality or condition of	condition of being happy	cleanliness
d.	together	the ability to get along	accompany, companion
e.	not	not agree	disappointment
f.	accomplish, perform	working well, working as intended	defect
g.	bend	able to change easily	reflex
h.	not	not patient	impersonal
i.	not	unwilling to make any changes	inappropriate
j.	between	communicate with someone	interrupt
k.	many	having different characteristics	multiply
l.	before	say beforehand	prehistoric
m.	say	something that tells what will happen	dictator, dictation
n.	mind	person who deals with personal issues	psychology
o.	person	person who studies science	chemist

Preparing to Write 2: Adding Support *(pages 100–101)*

2. *(pages 100–101)*
a. 2; b. 1; c. 1, 2, 3; d. 1, 2, or 3; e. 1

Preparing to Write 3: Writing Introductions and Conclusions *(pages 101–103)*

1. *(pages 102–103)*
b. surprising fact; c. description of a scene; d. question; e. relevant quotation

Editing and Rewriting: More Editing for Articles *(page 104)*

These items require articles: e. the; h. a; p. a; s. the or no article; t. an; u. a

4 Surfing the Web

CHAPTER 9

Reading 1 *(pages 108–112)*

2. *(pages 110–111)*

	Meaning	*Context clues*
WWW	World Wide Web	parentheses
surfing the Web	browsing of the Internet	definition ("is called")
home pages	starting points for the Web user	comma
html	hypertext mark-up language	parentheses
URL address	Uniform Resource Locator	parentheses
domain	a group of computers that share the same common suffix	parentheses
FAQs	frequently asked questions	parentheses
America Online	an on-line service	such as
user-friendly	not hard to read, not taking a lot of the user's time to download	contrast with following sentences
navigationally clear	easy to move around in	hyphen

3. *(page 112)*
a. 3; b. 5; c. 6; d. 1; e. 7; f. 4; g. 2

Reading 2 *(pages 112–115)*

2. *(page 114)*
a. F; b. T; c. T; d. F; e. T; f. F
3. *(pages 114–115)*
a. Chinese; b. two-thirds; c. nearly equal to that of; d. nearly; e. more than a

Reflect on Reading *(page 115)*

Second sentence

Targeting: Internet Expressions *(pages 115–116)*

1. *(pages 115–116)*
b. computer, ways Internet users can communicate with each other; c. off-line, being connected to the Internet; d. word processing, ways to describe "the Internet"; e. users, companies that offer Internet connection service; f. modems, what you can find on a home page
2. *(page 116)*
a. 2; b. 1; c. 2; d. 1; e. 2; f. 2; g. 2; h. 1; i. 2; j. 2

CHAPTER 10

Reading 1 *(pages 118–122)*

2. *(page 121)*
a. 6; b. 5; c. 4; d. 8; e. 2; f. 3; g. 7; h. 1
3. *(pages 121–122)*
a. because it's easy to meet people and to overcome shyness; b. a person can grow and become less inhibited; c. someone on-line could be dangerous or deceptive; d. don't give out personal identification information too soon and treat everyone with respect; e. click on the mouse to send someone a private message; f. a picture of flowers on the Internet (a person gets an e-mail message to visit a web site where there is a bouquet of flowers and a message for him or her)

Reading 2 *(pages 122–123)*

2. *(page 123)*
a. 1; b. 4; c. 9; d. 2; e. 8; f. 6; g. 10; h. 3; i. 5; j. 7

Targeting: Expressions for "Said" (pages 124–125)

a. told; b. exclaimed; c. argued; d. wondered; e. suggested; f. replied, told; g. wondered; h. confided; i. admitted; j. advised

Editing and Rewriting: Editing for Punctuation with Quotes (pages 126–127)

2. (pages 126–127)
a. ladies!"; b. (new paragraph) guys!"; c. (new paragraph) Evan, "I've . . . meeting."; d. (new paragraph) responded, "Me; e. ?"; f. (new paragraph) Internet," Lisa said, "but; g. (not a new paragraph); h. sighed, !"; i. (new paragraph) tomorrow,; j. you."; k. (not a new paragraph) delete the " at the beginning of the sentence

CHAPTER 11

Reading (pages 129–135)

3. (page 131)
II. Limits to free speech to protect citizens
    A. against libel
    B. common standards of decency
       1. obscenity
       2. blasphemy
       3. profanity
    C. Internal disorder or interference with the operation of the government
       1. treason
       2. failure to obey U.S. laws, violence, or other crimes
III. Attempts to limit free speech on the Internet
    A. Limitations on free speech from past legal decisions
       1. in newspapers
       2. in public places
    B. Debate about limiting free speech on the Internet
       1. Communications Decency Act
          a. designed to limit children's access to indecent materials on the Internet
          b. struck down by U.S. Supreme Court
       2. Opposition to regulation
          a. will stifle growth of new technology
          b. Internet thrives on diversity of thought
          c. parents can use computer programs to monitor or restrict children's access
       3. Parents' arguments
          a. pornography and explicit conversations on Internet damage health of society
          b. government regulation necessary to protect users
          c. do not trust high-tech companies to do this

4. (page 132)

b. libel [2]	making false written statements about someone	definition given ("Libel means . . .")
c. obscenity [3]	sexually explicit behavior, language, or material	parentheses
d. blasphemy	speaking disrespectfully against God	parentheses
e. profanity	using bad language	"or"
f. treason [4]	an action such as planning to overthrow the government	comma
g. struck down [6]	said was unconstitutional	"The court said . . . "
h. legislation [7]	an act of law of government	"such as"

5. (page 132)
a. obscenity; b. blasphemy; c. treason; d. profanity; e. libel
6. (pages 132–133)
a. opponents; b. connected with; c. stifle; d. thrives; e. diversity; f. medium; g. monitor; h. restrict; i. objectionable
7. (page 133)
a. restrictions; b. pornography; c. explicit; d. foolproof; e. regulations
9. (pages 133–135)
a. restricted; b. regulation; c. restrict; d. limit; e. limiting; f. regulate; g. objectionable; h. controls; i. protect; j. guarantee; k. protected; l. harmful; m. guaranteed; n. restricted; o. damaging; p. limited; q. limitation or limitations

5 Cityscapes

CHAPTER 12

Reading 1 (pages 143–147)

3. (pages 144–145)
a. schnoz; b. sneeze; c. sniff; d. Cyrano de Bergerac; e. snout; f. snort
4. (page 145)
a. 2; b. 3; c. 1
5. (page 145)
a. city; b. counter; c. city; d. city; e. counter
6. (page 146)
a. 3; b. 4
7. (page 146)
commercial use-3c, commercial area-2b, commercial value-4d, commercial intent-d.

Reading 2 (pages 147–152)

2. (page 150)
a. 1; b. 2; c. 2; d. 3; e. 2; f. 1
3. (pages 150–151)
a. will not
b. The towers do not look like what they were supposed to; it has four fat towers; it overpowers its surroundings
c. Books would be destroyed by exposure to strong sunlight; library workers would have to go up and down towers to get books for people in the basement
d. Shortened the towers, doubled the thickness of the towers' glass, and lined the towers with wood paneling
e. 1. Today volume equals meaning. 2. Finding the information
f. 2
4. (page 152)
positive comments: fine design; beyond simple functionality; farsighted; outstanding architectural project; provides access for researchers and the public; better use of public money
negative comments: cost exorbitant amount; worst choice to spend so much money; aesthetic value means nothing when talking about libraries; decision-making gone wrong/ignorant decision-making; on a flood plain; inexperienced architect; books with a view rather than people having view since they are on the lower floors; wooden shutters block light; landscaping project grander than necessary

CHAPTER 13

Reading (pages 158–166)

2. (page 161)
a. 2; b. 3; c. 1
3. (page 161)
a. 3; b. 1; c. 2; d. 5; e. 4
4. (pages 162–163)
Answers will vary. Sample answers:
b. People are isolated; they don't even know their neighbors' names; they don't feel committed to their community; they don't feel that they belong.

c. Neighborhoods are small; people know each other; things are very close and the style of the neighborhood is attractive, harmonious, and appealing.
d. Houses were not created to last for many years; they were built with cheap materials.
e. Things were not created to last long. People don't think about the future.
f. The street is an extension of the house. Windows face out so people can enjoy the life of the street.
g. Zoning laws regulate the use of an area, for example, whether someone can operate a business or build a tall building in an area. These laws put aspects of life into different areas. Business is separate from residential.
h. The business area goes on forever. It's not integrated into areas with civic and private structures.
i. The design is not created to match the size of people, but of large machines. It is impersonal.
j. It has no feeling, no personality.
k. Neighborhoods collectively grouped together make up a town.
l. Roads are like hallways connecting areas such as parks, nature preserves, travel routes, or railroad lines.
m. Cars are not as important as people and their needs. Less attention should be paid to parking areas and highways and more should be paid to building communities that have things close enough for people to walk to.
n. This code would restrict which styles people could use so that there was harmony in appearance.
5. (page 164)

Cause	Effect
no quaint neighborhoods	*loss of small-town friendliness*
everything is far away	*cars dominate our lives*
people have to drive everywhere; everything is far away; no small-town friendliness	a feeling of isolation, a lack of community, no sense of place
modern, inexpensive building materials and styles	*buildings not expected to last; buildings do not connect us with the styles of the past*
homes and businesses looked onto the street	*people could watch and participate in the life of the street*
need for security and privacy	homes designed to separate us from the "outdoor room"
zoning laws	commercial areas and residential areas separate
automobiles not permitted	*each neighborhood has a public bus stop*
recreating certain qualities of village life	*brings life back into urban areas*

Editing and Rewriting: Editing for Problems in Problem-Solution Writing (pages 172–174)

2. (pages 173–174)
a. and ground pollution
b. had not allowed
c. ~~we decide to make~~ or made into
d. if the planners had put . . .
e. effort to clean up
f. the city give
g. or building
h. make
i. would give

6 Closing the Loop: Recycling

CHAPTER 14
Starting Point (page 177)

3. (page 177)
Answers will vary. Possible answers:
We are using up our raw materials.
We are using up our energy sources.
The population is increasing so we have more energy needs and more garbage to dispose of.

Reading 1 (pages 177–179)

2. (page 178)
a. made with some recycled materials; b. can be recycled; c. completely made from recycled materials
3. (page 179)
a. Consumers keep the cycle going.
b. *Recyclable* means that something is able to be recycled. *Recycled* means that something is made with recycled material.
c. This will encourage them to buy recycled and recyclable materials also.
d. Recycled products save on natural resources and energy, conserve landfill space, and reduce pollution.
4. (page 179)
a. 4; b. 3; c. 5; d. 2; e. 1

Reading 2 (pages 180–183)

3. (pages 181–182)
a. They are sorted into paper grades.
b. It is sent to paper manufacturers.
c. They bleach it.
d. Hydrogen peroxide or sodium hydrosulfite is added.
4. (page 182)
They would dissolve in the pulping process.
5. (page 182)

Prefix	Meaning	From reading	Another example
de-	*out of*	de-inking process	*decay; desalinate*
re-	*again*	recycling, reusing	*review*
hydro-	*water*	sodium hydrosulfite	*hydroelectric; dehydrated*
di-	*two*	chlorine dioxide	*divide; divorce*
co-	*together*	collect	*collate; co-worker*
pre-	*before*	precycling	*preview*

6. (page 183)

Root	Meaning	From reading	Another example
cycle	*wheel, circle*	*recycled*	*bicycle*
duc	*lead*	*producing*	*conduct*
ology	*study of*	*technology*	*biology*
tech	*skill*	*technology*	*technique*
manu	*hand*	*manufacturers*	*manual*
fact	*make*	*manufacturers*	*factory*

7. *(page 183)*

newspapers, papermakers, groundwood, newsprint

Targeting: Process Terms *(pages 184–185)*

2. *passive:* is/are sorted into; is/are made into; is/are sent; is/are put into; is/are processed; is/are used; is/are collected by; is/are bleached
3. *(pages 184–185)*
a. consists of/involves; b. is put into; c. is sorted into; d. send; e. is processed; f. is made into; g. is used; h. use; i. uses; j. is made into

CHAPTER 15

Reading *(pages 189–195)*

3. *(pages 193–194)*
a. O; b. O; c. O; d. F; e. F; f. O; g. F; h. F; i. O; j. O; k. O; l. F; m. F; n. F
5. *(pages 194–195)*
a. recycled; b. confusing; c. burned; d. obsessed; e. imported; f. grass-covered; g. enduring; h. recycling

Targeting: Coherence Devices *(pages 195–198)*

2. *(pages 197–198)*
b. they; c. household; d. However; e. that/which; f. manufacture; g. *(no change)*; h. it; i. thus; j. it; k. does; l. though

Preparing to Write: Discussing the Issues *(pages 198–201)*

3. *(page 201)*
Answers will vary. Possible answers:
a. Recycling is Garbage, (John) Tierney; b. the focus on recycling is based on myths.; c. recycling does not save energy or money.; d. recycling consumes resources

Editing and Rewriting: Editing for Problems with Coherence *(pages 201–202)*

a. In the 1980s recycling was already happening voluntarily and profit*ably* without government intervention. *This* changed in 1978. Newspapers are to blame for unnecessarily alarming the public with the news of a garbage barge *which* was unable to find a dumpsite. The barge traveled thousands of miles, trying to unload *its* cargo of Long Islanders' trash. *This* journey had a strange effect on America, *producing* fears *that are* based on seven myths about the garbage crisis in the U.S.

b. Consider these questions: Does a 5-cent deposit on a soft drink help the environment? Yes, *it does*, but a 5-cent deposit on a soft drink is more expensive *to* collect than curbside recycling *is. Second*, are reusable cups and plates better than disposables? No, *they aren't.* It actually takes more energy to *manufacture and wash ceramic mugs.* According to Martin Hocking, *a chemist at the University of Victoria in British Columbia*, you would have to use a mug 1,000 times before *its* energy-consumption-per-use is equal to the cup. *Next*, should you recycle today's newspaper? *You probably shouldn't.* Recycling newsprint actually creates more water pollution than making new paper: for each ton of recycled newsprint that's produced, an extra 5,000 gallons of waste water are discharged. *Finally*, should you require cloth diapers rather than plastic *ones*? Environmentalists have given up on this. The cost-benefit analysis became too confusing.

Text Credits

Page 2: Reprinted from the *Money* website at
http://www.azcentral.com/business/jobs/1006hotjobs.html by special permission. Copyright 1998, Time Inc.

Page 3: Copyright 1997 The Seattle Times Company. Used by permission from The Seattle Times Company and the Cincinnati Enquirer/Perry Brothers.

Page 25: Americans with Disabilities Act.

Pages 29–31: Reprinted with permission of Knight-Ridder/Tribune Information Services.

Pages 39–40: Source: Paraphrased from *Getting to Yes: Negotiating Agreement Without Giving In* by Roger Fisher and William Ury. Copyright © by Houghton Mifflin Company.

Pages 47–48: Taken from the *Dear Abby* column by Abigail Van Buren. Copyright © Universal Press Syndicate. Reprinted with permission. All rights reserved.

Page 49: Reprinted with permission from **http://www.ahipubs.com**. Copyright © Alexander Hamilton Institute, Inc., 70 Hilltop Road, Ramsey, NJ 07446.

Pages 61–62: Copyright © 1990 by Deborah Tannen, Ph.D. By permission of William Morrow & Company, Inc.

Page 66: Excerpt from *Talking Power* by Robin Tolmach Lakoff. Copyright © 1990 by Robin Tolmach Lakoff. Reprinted by permission of BasicBooks, a subsidiary of Perseus Books Group, LLC.

Pages 66–67: First appeared in *Working Woman,* October, 1994. Written by Anne Roipe and Elsye Mall. Reprinted with the permission of MacDonald Communications Corporation. Copyright © 1998 by MacDonald Communications Corporation. Copyright © 1998 by MacDonald Communications Corporation. For subscriptions call 1-800-234-9675.

Pages 78–79: Source: Excerpts from "Scientists Search for Happiness in Genes" by Faye Flam. From Knight-Ridder/Tribune News Service, October 6, 1996. Copyright © 1996 the **Philadelphia Inquirer**. Distributed by Knight-Ridder/Tribune Information Services.

Pages 78–79: Source: Excerpts from "The Science of Happiness" by David G. Myers and Ed Diener. From *The Futurist,* Sept.-Oct. 1997 issue, v31 n5 pSR 1(7).

Pages 93–94: Source: Paraphrased from "Blood Will Tell: In Japan, Type 'AB' Spells Romance" by Kevin Sullivan. From *Washington Post,* December 30, 1995.

Page 108: Copyright © 1997 by Houghton Mifflin Company. All rights reserved. Used with permission.

Pages 118–121: Reprinted with permission from *Parade,* copyright © 1996, and Sandee Brawarsky.

Pages 122–123: Used by permission from MSNBC on the Internet.

Page 130: Source: Paraphrased from "Parents must face seamy side of Internet" by Leyla Kokmen and Danny Westneat from *Seattle Times,* June 27, 1997 issue, p. A2.

Pages 134–135: Copyright 1997 Seattle Times Company. Reprinted with permission from the editorial pages of March 29, 1997.

Page 144: Reprinted by permission of *The Wall Street Journal,* copyright © 1990 Dow Jones & Company, Inc. All rights reserved worldwide.

Page 148: Copyright © 1995, *Washington Post.* Reprinted with permission.

Page 149: Selection from "Volumes of Controversy" by Catharine Reynolds. Reprinted from the January, 1997 issue of *Gourmet* by permission of the author.

Pages 158–161: Paraphrased from "Home from Nowhere" by James Howard Kunstler. From *The Atlantic Monthly,* September 1996 issue, pp. 43–66.

Pages 159–160: "Home from Nowhere" by James Howard Kunstler. From *The Atlantic Monthly,* September 1996 issue, pp. 43–66. Reprinted by permission from James Howard Kunstler.

Page 178: University of Washington – Solid Waste Management Office, P.O. Box 355210, University of Washington, Seattle, WA 98105. Reprinted with permission. Page 181: University of Washington – Solid Waste Management Office, P.O. Box 355210, University of Washington, Seattle, WA 98105. Reprinted with permission. Pages 189–192: Copyright © 1996 by The New York Times Company. Reprinted by permission.

Photo Credits

Page 1: © Joel Gordon 1998. Page 37: Howard Grey/© Tony Stone Images. Page 76: © Dick Luria/FPG International. Page 106: © Susie Fitzhugh. Page 141: (left) © Jeff Greenberg/The Picture Cube, Inc.; (right) © Frank Siteman/Stock Boston. Page 142: (left) © Susie Fitzhugh; (center) "Range Spirit" by Rex Barrick. Photo by Clay Bush, courtesy of Sul Ross State University News and Publication Service; (right) "Torch Bearers," 1962, by Charles Umlauf. Photo courtesy of Mears Photography and Mrs. Charles Umlauf. Page 148: Michel Ginies/SIPA Press. Page 157: (left) © Aaron Strong/Gamma-Liaison Photo Agency; (right) © Kindra Clineff/The Picture Cube, Inc. Page 176: © Jim Corwin/Photo Researchers, Inc. Page 189: © Andrew Holbrooke/Gamma-Liaison Photo Agency.